STUDIO 804

Design Build Expanding the pedagogy of architectural education

STUDIO 804

Design Build Expanding the pedagogy of architectural education

Dan Rockhill
Text developed from interviews by David Sain

OSCAR RIERA OJEDA
PUBLISHERS

CONTENTS

01

INTRODUCTION

In addition to presenting the architecture of Studio 804 this book is my first-person account of the evolution of the program. I share an architectural experience that has found its way to success over the last 20+ years by navigating through the entanglements that thwart many well intended programs.

Project by project I share the way we operate. How the students approach the work, the methods of design and design development and the day to day engagement with the various institutional and community bodies that can often make or break a project. It is not just a book about design, or an educational model, it is also a book about the hard work and the determination it takes for anyone to produce architecture that not only teaches but inspires students as well as the public.

DAN ROCKHILL AND STUDIO 804

"Amateurs look for inspiration; the rest of us just get up and go to work",
Chuck Close, American painter/artist and photographer

LEAVING THE CLASSROOM

Yearly, since the Barber School was completed, Studio 804 has designed and built a project. I did not have a grand plan during those first years – the program was created on the run within the six-credit hour design studio I was teaching. Problems were solved as they presented themselves. We started by building a small artist's studio, a pavilion and then single-family houses close to the University of Kansas campus that focused on affordability and accessibility. Once the program had proven itself we started a series of prefabricated affordable houses in marginal neighborhoods in Kansas City, Kansas. Each year the students found the property and solicited the funding. These projects were done with the goal of seeding urban change through creative, modern solutions to the housing problems the city faced. These projects were widely recognized and significantly raised the profile of Studio 804. Now, after more than 20 projects, Studio 804 is a not-for-profit 501(c)3 corporation that operates as a full-year studio. It is a fully synthesized educational experience that focuses on the research and development of inventive building solutions that address pressing issues that face the built environment. Over the last decade, the emphasis has been the future of sustainable design and how new and emerging technologies can be combined with passive strategies to create the type of zero energy, resource neutral buildings that are likely to soon be necessary.

TECHNOLOGICAL CHANGE AND SUSTAINABLE LIVING

Throughout history, economic transformations occur when new communication technologies converge with new energy and transportation systems. At the turn of the 19th century abundant coal and steam power, combined with the telegraph and the railroad to feed the First Industrial Revolution. As we moved into the 20th century the Second Industrial Revolution came with wide spread access to electricity that made television, radio and the telephone possible, while cheap oil supported the internal combustion engine and the rise of cars and the highway system. Currently, new forms of social communication, renewable energies and smart transportation are giving rise to what is often being referred to as the Third Industrial Revolution[1]. I do not necessarily believe we will see the economic future often associated with this idea, but I do believe these technologically driven concepts will shape the future of architecture as global climate change continues to impact how we live on a crowded planet with limited resources. It is important to train students to be prepared to take part in, or even lead these changes.

Graduating architects will need to be comfortable working with the infrastructure of this new digital community that will increasingly connect everyone and everything in an expanding network. In the "Internet of Things" people, machines, vehicles, road systems, homes, offices, manufacturing lines, the electrical grid, almost every aspect of economic and social life, will be connected[2]. This has the potential to create an efficient flow of energy and goods that will target need and promote a smart, green digital economy where the production and use of energy and resources is managed fairly and shared rather than centralized and sold. An example of these change in action is in Germany where 25 percent of the electricity powering the country comes from people using renewable energies to turn their buildings into micro power plants. They are targeting 35 percent by 2020[3]. In a shared economy, these micro power plants will use the internet of things to distribute the energy to everyone's advantage through a smart, localized energy infrastructure.

The work Studio 804 has done the last 10 years looks to this future. Most of the students who make up my class are conscious of their role as stewards of the planet and are deeply concerned about fairness across societies. Unlike people my age who have spent their lives carving out what is theirs the younger generations are much more willing to be part of a shared economy. They are more concerned about access than ownership and are ready to embrace the daily use of technology. They already share music, television, news, etc. across the digital economy.

An example of the impact this might have is seen in the changes being brought to the world of transportation. College students are interested in doing more than adding charging stations and targeted parking for alternative vehicles. Many of them see transportation the same way they see music, they want to use their smartphones to immediately contact and pay Uber or Lyft for access to mobility rather than be tethered to their own vehicle. There is no reason to see why these atti-

1) The idea of the Third Industrial Revolution is commonly associated with the writings of Jeremy Rifkin (American, 1945), economic and social theorist. His books include *The Third Industrial Revolution* (2011, St. Martin's Griffin) and *The Zero Marginal Cost Society: The Internet of Things, the Collaborative Commons, and the Eclipse of Capitalism* (2014, St. Martin's Griffin).

2) The Internet of Things is a term coined by Kevin Ashton (United Kingdom, 1968), the technology pioneer who co-founded the Auto-ID Center at the Massachusetts Institute of Technology that develops new technologies for revolutionizing global commerce. He is the author of the book *How to Fly a Horse, The Secret History of Creation, Invention and Discovery* (2015, Anchor).

3) Rifken, Jeremy, *"The Rise of the Internet of Things and the Race to Zero Marginal Cost Society"*, Part 1, The website The World Post, a partnership of The Huffington Post and the Berggruen Institute, October 26, 2015, updated on November 26, 2016.

A
___
B C

A *Mod 3 is one of the prefabricated affordable houses Studio 804 built in marginal neighborhoods in Kansas City, Kansas in the mid 2000's. The four Mod projects increased the programs profile.*

B *The preservation of the Barber School was the first project completed by Studio*

804. It was a one-time effort done to help a terminally ill colleague finish a project. It did not take long to notice the enthusiasm the students had for getting their hands in the wet concrete, welding steel and building what had started out as an idea on paper. I have not stopped building with students since.

C *One of the latest completed Studio 804 project is a zero-energy use LEED Platinum certified house. The program now focuses on these high-performance standards.*

DAN ROCKHILL AND STUDIO 804

tudes will not continue to expand further into the economy and our shared infrastructure.

To operate in this new economic environment there will be a greater need for integrated thinking. Architects will need to holistically understand the world within which they work to be able to design and build buildings that respond to a highly connected and shared world. The architecture profession must continue to shake off the decades of specialization and address a complex web of issues, both virtual and material, to create good buildings. To do this I think the profession needs to look back to how buildings were produced before specialization and risk management reduced the role of the architect in the 20th century. We should see ourselves as high-tech master builders who oversee the entire process. Someone who understands this is the Finnish architect, author, and philosopher, Juhani Pallasmaa. His works and writings have always inspired me. He may be referring to a different era in architecture and technology, but the thoughts are timeless.

> In an interview when Pallasmaa was asked if he sees himself as an architect he responded, "I have been a farm-hand, a construction worker, an administrator, a university rector, a graphic and product designer, etc. But I do everything through an architect's eyes and mind set. However, I don't mean architect as a professional, but as an archetype, a '-smith,' as it were. A blacksmith would not be a professional, but almost a mythical person. In the same way, I regard an architect as a supporter of the mythical dimensions of life, not a professionalist".

> When asked about the tension between the personal experience and creating universal design he added, "I cannot separate them in any fundamental sense. Ludwig Liechtenstein writes, 'I am my world.' If you think that way, you can't separate things. And I don't believe all things need to be separated. I think today there's too much of that categorization as an intellectual game. For instance, one's sense of existence absolutely calls for the simultaneous acknowledgment of self and the world, doesn't it? There is no existence unless the two dimensions fuse into one".[4]

4) Juhani Pallasmaa is a Finnish architect, author, philosopher, critic and former dean at the Helsinki University of Technology. His comments are from an interview with Andrew Caruso done in 2011 during Pallasmaa's time as professor in residence and 2011 Walton Critic at The Catholic University of America. It was published on the website of the National Building Museum, Washington DC. *"Interview with an Architectural Icon: Juhani Pallasmaa"*.

D *The students have finished projects of a size and complexity that I would not have dreamed possible in 1995 - including The Forum at Marvin Hall - an addition to the School of Architecture and Design building at the University of Kansas. It was completed in 2014 and is the largest and most complex project we have finished. The exterior facade is wrapped with a dual wall. It communicates with a roof top weather station and an array of sensors and dampers that allow it to adapt to the immediate conditions, so the building can operate at peak efficiency in heating, cooling and daylighting.*

EXPERIENTIAL LEARNING

Experiential learning is the process of learning by doing and then reflecting upon this action to apply it to new problems. I see this method of teaching as particularly applicable to architecture. Students are challenged to creatively solve interrelated concrete problems and each decision creates a new set of interrelated problems to be addressed. There are limitations to teaching in a classroom and this type of learning is best served in an apprenticeship like situation. To quote Peter Buchanan, integrated thinking can be more successfully taught "by letting the student work with someone who has mastered the skills, who knows how to think with his/her fingers and mind, drawing on both conscious skills and what has become unconscious bodily knowledge, so integrating head, hand and heart".[5]

In Studio 804 these experiential lessons go well beyond the simple installation of materials as the students learn to work with others and orchestrate all the moving parts that go into a building. The students are with me for complex meetings where wall assemblies, ventilation strategies, and digital communications systems are discussed, debated and eventually integrated into the design. The students are then on site and involved in directly installing these systems. This education is not unlike doing a medical residency before becoming a practicing doctor. It makes as little sense to have architecture graduates who sees the idea of displacement ventilation as a mystery as it does to have a graduating doctor who does not know how the lungs work.

HANDS-ON

From the moment a Studio 804 class first gathers much of the work is hands-on. Even the design phase includes mock-ups and experiments (as well as working with the latest Building Information Modelling and other computer technologies to produce drawings, renderings, and construction documents). They work with me on everything; excavation, pouring concrete, framing walls, welding steel, laying masonry, installing roofing, making flashings, and setting windows and doors. They run plumbing lines and set fixtures, work on the mechanical systems, and run the wire. In short, there is little about building that the students won't have a chance to experience for themselves. Building this way allows the studio to pursue new ideas and develop unique details that might ordinarily be presumed too costly. Typically, as the number of trades increases so does the budget. I see Studio 804 as a one-stop-shop where all trades are on site from the beginning, so everything remains in house and manageable.

As a project is developed the students are divided into building divisions, they step forward and volunteer to oversee concrete, finishes, plumbing, bookkeeping, etc. They develop ideas and contacts for their division and then report to the group where decisions are finalized as a studio. Each student is expected to fully immerse themselves in their subject so that they can fluently communicate the applicable concepts with the rest of the class, the clients, the public or any professionals it might involve.

DESIGN

The design work is done collaboratively and is as democratic as possible. For every stage and scale of design all the students are encouraged to present concepts for consideration and I take the strengths of the individual ideas and discuss them with the group in a way that begins to make everyone feel involved. It becomes a shell game where I move this idea here, that one there – the first idea re-emerging but now as part of someone else's idea until we get to a point where no one is sure where anything originated.

I have become less patient with the earliest parts of this process. I am now more open with my ideas when it comes to shaping the design concept. In the design studios the students have before joining Studio 804 the schematic concept is over emphasized. I want them to learn the importance of design development. I feel it is more likely to lead to memorable architecture than the overall design concept. There are still layers of design work for the student to engage in, they have to learn to embrace the opportunities. There are many examples throughout the book of this evolution.

The goal is to finish each building by graduation in May, but this does not always happen. When we do go long I have to convince students to delay job hunting, or starting their jobs, or travelling the world, to see the project through to the finish. It is usually evident quite early when this is going to happen and I get the students to commit before they have a full grasp of how ready they will be to stop showing up at the job site six days a week at 7am. Even when the construction is finished on schedule there is still much to be done since the rest of world does not run on a school year schedule. For example, the students who do the LEED certification and keep the books typically remain active well into the summer or even the next school year to finish their responsibilities and assure that the next year's class will not have to pick up their work.

NATURE DEFICIT DISORDER

To do this work with inexperienced students who have spent much of their lives indoors is a daunting task. A 2005 Kaiser Family Foundation study found that youth between the 7th and 12th grade spent an average of eight and a half hours a day with electronic media.[6] This was the same year Richard Louv published, "Last Child in the Woods". He argued that behavioral problems can be linked to the decline in time spent outdoors. It is there, a person better learns to adapt to the unpredictably of life.[7]

5) Buchanan, Peter, "The Big Rethink Part 9: Rethinking Architectural Education", The Architectural Review, September 28, 2012.

6) The Henry J. Kaiser Family Foundation, A Kaiser Family Foundation, "Generation M: Media in the Lives of 8-18 Year-Olds" March 2005, pp 38.

7) Louv, Richard, Last Child in the Woods, Saving Our Children from Nature-Deficit Disorder. United States of America, Algonquin Books of Chapel Hill, 2005, Louv writes about the issues related to mental health in chapter 4, "Climbing the Tree of Health" pp 44. and engaging an unpredictable world is discussed in chapter 10, "Scared Smart: Facing the Bogeyman, pp 176.

E F
G H

E F *From beginning to end the Studio 804 experience is hands-on. The students are challenged to learn a variety of trades and then implement them in the design and construction of the project. They do research, contact suppliers, work on mock-ups and then are on site doing the final installation. They not only learn to work with new technologies such as the rainscreen membrane used in the EcoHawks woven cladding but also learn the traditional method of assembly such as soldering.*

G *Anyone who works with Studio 804 is primarily working with the students. They represent the program at all meetings. This photo was taken during a presentation to the people of Greensburg, Kansas while working on the first public building finished after a tornado destroyed the city.*

H *Throughout design and design development the students are put in a position where they do not feel they are competing against each other. The process is calibrated to assure that the final design will not be thought of as a single student's vision. If resentment over the design can fester the project will suffer.*

I J
K

The sheltered youth he described are now college students. When they join Studio 804 and start working on site it awakens a sensory connection between them and their surroundings that has atrophied during an upbringing that devalues physical encounters with nature or even the urban streets. This subconscious sensory training during childhood once placed a foundation under an architectural education that has become even more virtual and detached from the physical world.

The students are often blind to many of the subtle possibilities of an architecture based on experience rather than appearance alone. It is usually easier to get them to embrace the building's energy performance and social role than it is to fully embrace the tectonics. As sustainable design has become a requirement for more architectural projects and a demand from many clients it has become acceptable for architecture to be judged by energy performance alone. I want the experiential, the tectonic and the

poetic qualities of the building to be in the forefront of the user's mind. The responsible performance of the building should be an expectation, experiencing the building should make life richer.

THE MERITS OF HARD WORK

It is not always a pleasant experience for the students as I push them to work harder and accomplish more than they likely have ever been asked to do. They are engaged intellectually, emotionally, socially and physically and they learn not only by doing but by reflecting on doing. All problem solving is a process that includes numerous successes and failures. Rather than crumbling the first time they meet resistance the students learn to absorb these lessons and through reflection transfer them to new problems - strengthening skills and truly learning from experience. The students profit beyond the obvious fact that marketable skills are developed. They must learn to solve problems with their minds and bodies and to overcome the disconnect many are likely to

I J K *Every year, upon completion of the project, there is a day-long stream of people coming to see the work at an open house. The pride is evident on the faces of the students as they guide people through the projects and see the amazed reactions to what they have been able to do.*

feel between the two. They not only have to do manual work as well as solve objective building problems, but they also overcome the challenges of cold weather numbing their fingers, exhaustion making it hard to think or mud pulling at their boots and making everything slippery and difficult. I do not think it is antiquated to believe that overcoming these hardships makes for a stronger person – not by simply being tough enough to tolerate discomfort – but by having the resolve to see yourself through a difficult time and succeed. The greatest joy of my teaching is seeing an individual student, who struggles initially, who cannot come to terms with working with concrete or walking on joists or understanding that wood has a grain, become, over time, so confident in what they are doing that they see me as simply in the way.

FUNDING

It is a difficult time for many universities. As government funding is cut, institutions are looking for creative ways to support wor-

thy research. Studio 804 acts as a business and does not cost the University of Kansas anything beyond the cost of the warehouse where we work. Occasionally, I will agree to do work for a client but increasingly we develop and fund our own projects - which must be finished on budget and if they are speculative they need to be sold quickly since each year's class starts with nothing but the bank balance left by the previous year's class. The students are involved in all the negotiations and meetings in which they try to convince people to support the proposed work, help fund it, or once they have a project, allow it to start (usually in less time than the typical permitting and approvals process takes). I make sure it is known that anyone who works with Studio 804 is primarily working with the students - not me. I only step in when I feel it is necessary. This book will, project by project, describe the evolution of the business and how the efforts of the students change as the goals of the program change and I learn by experience.

02

BUILDING WITH STUDENTS

Before I started what has now become Studio 804 I required students to work with their hands in my design studios and a building technology practicum. They built intricate models, pieces of furniture and when the opportunity presented itself even more involved projects like a newspaper stand and a speaker's platform.

I had also been working with students in my design/build firm Rockhill and Associates where I hired them for manual labor and then, if they stayed and learned, allowed them to take on greater responsibility. These experiences prepared me for building with un-skilled but eager students. I had to be ready to push them to overcome several physical and mental chal-lenges in a very short time so they could solve the necessary problems to finish these early projects.

ROCKHILL AND ASSOCIATES

The One-Stop-Shop

EXPERIENCE

For several years before I started building with Studio 804 I had been working with a small crew doing unique projects throughout Kansas. These Rockhill and Associates projects were important in preparing me for the demands of Studio 804. It allowed me to develop the construction and management skills necessary to run a project with students.

After moving to Kansas with a young family and beginning to teach at the University of Kansas I started to supplement my income with this work. I had some building experience from my time in New York and had grown up comfortable with manual labor. I was drawn to the idea of architecture as a craft with a long tradition that had equally embraced design and construction. I started by working as a general contractor and slowly moved toward the one-stop-shop delivery method of Rockhill and Associates and then Studio 804.

In those early years, we worked on new houses and renovations, we restored outbuildings and barns, and took on whatever small unique work we could find. The crew was a mix of ages and experience that sometimes included my two sons. I also cycled through students from the architectural school who wanted a short-term building experience to add to their resume. Typically, they had no experience in building and often no experience with manual labor. I had the tools to do the work of several trades and with each project I was learning to manage a job site. I had always been curious about different building techniques and enjoyed the challenge of the new. For better or worse, Rockhill and Associates was not daunted by the responsibilities and risks that come with learning on the job.

One of the earliest challenges was the construction of a concrete belvedere on a hilltop in rural Kansas that overlooks the Wakarusa River. The owners wanted a weekend retreat that would be built to resist vandalism and would be reminiscent of the Pawnee Indian hogans they admired. This meant that they were not only asking for a concrete structure, but also that it be round. I had not worked with concrete beyond simple foundations and sidewalks and probably could have convinced them to take another path but instead accepted the challenge and began to figure out how it could be done.

The finished structure has an open plan with a central fire pit. The interior is sheltered from the north wind by the slope of the land and the solid concrete walls. It opens through large doors to the south facing slope and allows the winter sun to penetrate the space and keep it warm. During the summer the higher sun angles and the abundant foliage assure the interior is shaded and cool. The round form is sheltered with a cast-in-place concrete dome that spans 26 feet and is only three inches thick when it reaches the oculus. The greatest challenge was building the basket weave of wood shoring built with dimension lumber that supported the dome during the concrete pour. The finished structure won an American Concrete Institute award for excellence in concrete solutions and was an important step in transitioning Rockhill and Associates into more than a side job.

Rockhill and Associates developed into a full-time architecture and building LLC and became a model of the one-stop-shop approach that I have continued to this day with Studio 804. We were responsible for every step of the building process the law would allow and on the others, we worked with the electrical or mechanical subcontractors, so we could do as much of the work as possible while they confirmed it was done correctly and signed off.

Building our own projects was not just a choice and a matter of pride. It was a necessity. The buildings we were doing were unlike anything else being built in the region and often used materials in uncommon ways. The bidding process and labor costs would have led to budgets our clients could not support – assuming a contractor willing to bid on the work could even be found. If we would have tried to work in the traditional design-bid-build model, we would have had to compromise on much of the design work. It also would have removed much of the on-site spontaneity that was important to the work. We had a design phase and did a set of construction documents (hand drafted in the early days) but there was space left for custom hands-on problem solving and on site (or shop) improvisation that led to solutions that would have been hard to imagine at the desk.

A
___
   B

A *The Rockhill and Associates crew during months living in the Smoky Hills region in western Kansas. We were working on the preservation of Cottonwood Ranch, a state historic site. We have worked on many of the historic sites in Kansas.*

B *This concrete belvedere was one of Rockhill and Associates first projects and was an example of the advantages offered by the one-stop-shop approach to design as it creates the freedom to solve many detail problems on site as the work is being done.*

C   D E

THE MACKIE HOUSE

In the days before sustainability was a common term associated with architecture Rockhill and Associates was practicing some of the ideas. Along with using passive heating and cooling strategies we quite often sought out and used salvaged materials. We regularly searched the local wrecking yards and were in contact with regional demolition contractors looking for materials we could use or stockpile for later.

In 1989, the Mackie's were a young couple with two children who were hoping to build a house. They had a nice piece of rural land, about $50,000 and were open to experimentation. To make this house feasible it was decided to use salvaged materials in every possible way. In the 1980s these materials could be had for a few bucks or for free to those willing to go to the demolition site and remove them themselves. In the years since, sustainable design and the search for LEED credits have led to a stronger market for reclaimed materials. Supply and demand has created higher prices.

The University of Kansas was updating one of the science buildings and we were given permission to remove some of the old laboratory cabinetry ourselves. We used these for the kitchen cabinets. The room dividers were made with salvaged steel industrial window frames filled with reclaimed ribbed glass. The railings were made with used steel decking. Throughout the interior, we used salvaged industrial ladders, bathroom fixtures, steel stair stringers and even a steel pipe that became a "fire pole". It was for the kids to use to slide down from the parent's loft bedroom to theirs below.

On the exterior salvaged materials allowed for higher quality finishes than would have been otherwise possible on such a limited budget. The siding used is a heavy gauge corrugated aluminum that we were given permission to remove from the roof of an abandoned building that was to soon be demolished at a local fertilizer plant. We also used honed Virginia greenstone that we removed from another University of Kansas building as preparations were being made for an addition.

Working on the Mackie house helped me learn to creatively adapt to these salvaged materials and incorporate them into a design. It also allowed me to strengthen my connections with the salvage yards and demolitions contractors who would notify me when a good opportunity presented itself to collect unique or high-quality materials. These methods of procuring and using salvaged materials were a common part of the early Studio 804 projects.

C *The Mackie House was done for a small budget using salvaged and reclaimed materials whenever possible. The most conspicuous salvaged component are the thirty-foot steel fink trusses that were taken from a demolished railroad building. They were the impetus behind the design and supported the roof that spans over a flexible open plan.*

D E *All our work, be it a commissioned sculpture such as the one above, or a new house and art studio such as the one above incorporated several custom-made components in which we used readily available materials to create unique features that set the work apart from typical construction. The sculpture extensively used off the shelf galvanized threaded pipe and accessories to create an inexpensive armature to hold the glass. The house is sided with precast concrete panels we poured on site.*

HISTORIC STRUCTURES

Rockhill and Associates started as supplemental income but by the early 1990s had become a full-time business with a crew of workers dependent upon a year-round pay check. It was hard to meet even our limited payroll with the design of new houses. Building houses is always a difficult way to make a living but it is even more difficult when the projects are done for little money and are experimental in nature. We have always tended to put ambition over profit. To address this problem, we started working on historic buildings in Kansas. We had stumbled into this through the rehabilitation of a state registered historic house in Lawrence. A local preservation group had saved the house from demolition, got it listed and then had to find a way to make the property financially viable. This was before the housing boom of the 1990s when it would have been an easier task; a few years later people started moving back into the old neighborhood

and property values started raising. The Benedict House was on a double lot and we were asked to frugally design and build apartments that would convert the historic house into a hub surrounded by new rental units. All, without destroying it historic character. The results were unique and clearly new while still respecting the older architecture.

The one-stop-shop was appealing to the State Historic Preservation Office (SHPO) who had to maintain these sites. We had the tools, equipment, skills and willingness to tackle whatever task was at hand. We travelled to the site, stayed in local motels or bed and breakfasts and did everything – there was rarely a need for anyone else to work on the site. This approach made the jobs easier to coordinate as there were fewer entities involved. The work often required on-site decision making and we could work with the state offices to quickly determine a solution and keep the effort on schedule. Soon, we were the go to crew for this type of work in Kansas. When I started Studio 804 Rockhill and Associates had won a dozen Kansas Preservation Alliance Awards for excellence.

This work was a chance to hone skills and figure out the solutions for several unique problems. For example, we prepared a handful of historic structures to be temporarily moved or lifted so we could repair, underpin or replace the existing foundations. We would find ways to stabilize the structures without doing permanent damage and then would work with regional house movers to lift or move the buildings we had prepared. One of these was one of the few Pony Express Stations still standing in America. We restored it and now it is a museum near Hollenberg, Kansas. We also restored a cypress wood stave water tower built in 1885 at the southern end of the flint hills to serve locomotives. We preserved Constitution Hall in Lecompton, Kansas which became a museum dedicated to the "bleeding Kansas" era of the state's history and we worked extensively on two historic masonry projects. One was Cottonwood Ranch, an early sheep ranch in Kansas that was operated by an English immigrant who was an early proponent of photography and left a substantial record of the ranch's history. It is now a museum dedicated to the settlement of the region. The other was the restoration of the blockhouse at Fort Hays State Historical Site in Hays, Kansas. The blockhouse was the defensive strong point for the fort that was built during the American Indian Wars when the quickly growing American nation collided with the traditions and attempts of the Plains Indians to survive. It was built to protect the railroad workers and provide supplies to other forts not served by the railroad. This project included the replacing of the lower courses of limestone on the outer wythe that had deteriorated beyond repair. SHPO had records that located the original quarry used during the construction of the fort and permission was given for Rockhill and Associates to return to the site and extract the stone needed for the replacement work.

If not for this work done with the Rockhill and Associates crew it would have been much more difficult to manage those early Studio 804 years. We had tackled such a wide variety of projects and building techniques that when I started working with students I was comfortable operating a one-stop-shop that took on about any building challenge.

```
F    H K
  G    I L
       J
```

F The Benedict House preservation and the construction of the new "cottages" helped save the historic house in a Lawrence neighborhood that was being damaged by the demolition of older houses to replace them with poorly built student apartments. The National Park Service used it as a model for how to approach additions to historic buildings. It gave us the resume to start working on historic properties throughout the state of Kansas.

G We travelled to Beaumont, Kansas, lived in a closed hotel and spent the days restoring a cypress stave water tower that had served the railroad at the end of the 19th century.

H The restoration of the Hollenberg Pony Express Station in northern Kansas included temporarily moving the building so we could underpin the stone foundation that had been simply sitting on the grade. We poured reinforced concrete footings and then re-laid the visible stone foundation. Each stone returned to its documented location.

I Constitution Hall in Lecompton, Kansas is a significant site in pre-civil war American history and the battles over Kansas' entry to the union as free or slave state. We lifted the building to underpin and repair its deteriorated foundation. Afterwards, we fully preserved the building and even designed and built the display cases for the museum.

J The Fort Hays Block House in Hays, Kansas.

K L The Rockhill and Associates crew quarried stone from the original quarry sites while restoring the Fort Hays Block House in Hays, Kansas and Cottonwood Ranch near Hill City. We approached the work much as it had been done over 100 years before using sledge hammers and steel wedges to break free the stone needed and then dressed it on site to match the surfacing of the existing stone.

M *Rockhill and Associates designed and built a temporary wedding chapel using downed trees in the woods surrounding the site.*

STUDIO AND SHOP WORK,
1980-1994

Marvin Hall, University of Kansas

HAND AND MIND

From my first days of teaching at the University of Kansas I was determined to have students work with their hands and mind. I wanted to emphasize the tectonics of design and how design could evolve from the materials as much as the concept.

In my building technology practicum as well as my design studios I had students building objects. In my practicum they worked in the Marvin Hall shop or the building yard to construct their designs. They built all sorts of furniture and objects that taught them the process of converting an idea to reality. Eventually the students were working cooperatively to build objects for campus such as the newspaper stand in front of Marvin Hall.

In my design studio, this process took the shape of a series of model building projects. I felt then, as I do now, that too many design studios overwhelm the student with large and complex design programs – often adding layers of social activism, that

while honorable creates another layer of study that removes the students form the more pragmatic aspects of building. They end up spending most of their time trying to solve the complexities of the program and the building's mission statement. They then try to wrap it in some sort of attractive shell - often exhibiting a current architectural trend.

I did not want students spending time solving the problems of complex adjacencies. I devised a series of design problems that remove the work from typical functional requirements and preconceived notions. We designed objects that would physically represent harmony or rhythm. I wanted to keep it abstract, so they put their energy into designing the forms and resolving intricate material connections. If we designed what could be construed as a building it would be a fire fighter's practice tower or a meditation room for the Flint Hills in Kansas. We used balsa wood, soldered various metals, poured concrete bases and built intricate structures to realize the designs.

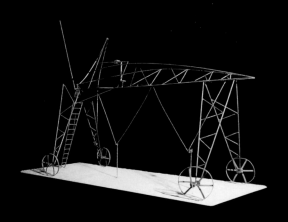

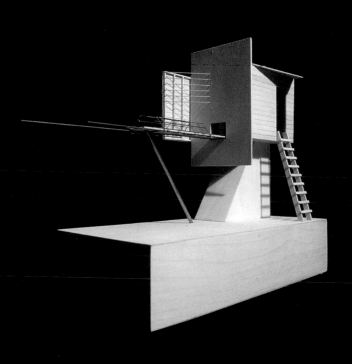
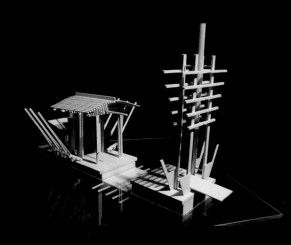
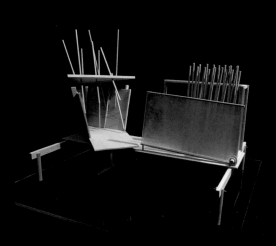

THE BARBER SCHOOL, 1995

Clinton Lake State Park, Lawrence, Kansas

ARCH 804

In 1995 I was teaching the final design studio, ARCH 804, in the graduate school at the University of Kansas. This can be a difficult class; the students often have one foot out the door and are focused on their portfolios and finding a job, not on another semester of paper architecture. At best, I hoped for the student's divided attention.

HARRIS STONE

Harris Stone, a preservationist and fellow professor in the Architecture program at the University of Kansas had spent summers working with students to stabilize the Barber School ruins; the remains of a small stone structure built in 1872 about 15 minutes from the University of Kansas campus in what is now the Clinton Lake State Park.

Harris had offered a study abroad experience from 1982-1992 that worked each summer rebuilding portions of an expansive Italian Villa in Siena, Italy. It was the Spannocchia Preservation Program and he was the director. When he was back home for summers the Barber School became a laboratory for him to teach historic building techniques and an appreciation for the buildings of the rural Kansas landscape. With the help of the Lawrence Preservation Alliance, his plan was to eventually restore the entire school house.

This effort came to a stop when Harris was diagnosed with a terminal illness. This development shocked me. Like many others who knew him I wanted to do something to help. I knew the work on the Barber School was important to him, so I proposed finishing the restoration with my 1995 design studio. This way Harris could see the work completed.

HISTORIC STRUCTURES

When I arrived in Kansas in 1980 I began to photograph the historic and vernacular structures on the landscape of my new home. I was, and still am, interested in modern interpretations of these traditional building techniques and designs. I work under the belief that when you add to a historic structure the new work should be distinctly new. If you begin to blur this line you run the risk of cheapening the old as everything becomes part of a skin deep historic stage set and nothing is perceived as a true artifact. With Rockhill and Associates I had been faced with these design issues as we had done additions to, or built adjacent structures to historic buildings.

With this approach in mind my ARCH 804 class proposal would repair the rest of the Barber School's masonry walls as they existed – not filling in the voids where stone was missing - and then build a new, very light steel frame roof that would be completely independent of the existing structure. It was designed to sway gently in the wind like the grasses that surrounded the site and to be in stark contrast to the heavy stone walls. It would be a sheltered outdoor room, surrounded by stone and protected from the sun and rain. There was push back from some of the students who had worked on the project with Harris and had a more conservative view of how preservation work should be done. They wanted to see a full reconstruction of the school house with a roof, windows and doors that mimicked the original. To do this would take many semesters of work and much fund raising. Me and my students were working on a solution that could be completed in weeks for limited funds.

Our solution had the support from the Lawrence Preservation Alliance, but obviously I felt it was imperative that Harris be on board with what we intended to do. The students produced a design model and steel mock-ups of the roof design. I wheeled it into the hospital to show Harris. He gave his full support and I felt comfortable proceeding in the face of any further resistance.

WORKING IN THE FIELD

It did not take long to see how enthused the students were about doing this work. Rather than falling asleep in the middle of the day in studio they were figuring out how to surround the Barber School with their cars, so they could use the headlights when darkness fell to finish the work the work they had started that day. They learned that working with concrete often takes more time than the short springs days allow. They did not have the experience to foresee this and to have lights and a generator on hand.

Something I saw that day and have seen through the years of Studio 804 is that students might not know how certain things are done but that is not always a bad thing. At the time Rockhill and Associates was building unique structures that required everyone involved to think unconventionally. When we looked to sub-contractors to help us solve problems or we hired an experienced worker who felt he or she knew the ways of building they would often act as if the work was being done wrong rather than helping think creatively. Many students don't have these ingrained beliefs and habits. Everything is new, and everything requires a creative solution. This might not always be efficient, but it can be refreshing.

When the Barber School was finished that spring, we had an on-site graduation ceremony and the students felt they had been involved in something important. Not only did it influence their thinking about the profession they were getting ready to enter but it changed my thoughts about how it can be taught. I knew I did not want to go back to prodding sleepy students to produce one last semester's worth of architectural images that they may or may not add to their portfolios.

A *The students designed, fabricated and installed a light steel frame to support corrugated roofing that hovers over the stone ruins to create a gazebo of sorts. It gently sways in the wind like the grasses that surround the school house.*

McCREA STUDIO, 1996

Rural Douglas County, Kansas

BUILDING AGAIN

The 1996 ARCH 804 studio had seen and heard about the Barber School experience and when they met in January they were asking to do something similar. They were not the only ones thinking this way. Remembering how engaged the students were at the Barber School and contrasting it with the detached efforts of my prior studios I was motivated to do it again. I started looking for a small project they could design and build and have finished at the end of the semester.

JUDY McCREA

Judy McCrea was the director of the Art Department at the University of Kansas and she had been mulling over the idea of a one room studio on a piece of property she owned twenty minutes from the University of Kansas campus in Lecompton, Kansas. She and I had casually discussed it as a future Rockhill and Associates project whenever she felt ready to proceed. No plans had been made. I approached her about working with my students and she was interested, but still did not have the money to build a finished studio. She felt comfortable that she could pay for the necessary materials to at least get started toward her eventual goal of a fully conditioned art studio. The students would build the unconditioned shell on a simple foundation that allows her the opportunity to get out of the weather while enjoying her property and doing her art. She would then finish the building over the years as funds permitted. This gave the students the opportunity to set the course for the overall design. They were charged with locating the building, developing its plan, giving it form, designing the foundation and determining the exterior finishes.

There was a meeting at the property to discuss the pros and cons of various locations for Judy's studio. I insisted that it be done in a manner consistent with the vernacular traditions of Kansas and not be built on tillable land. In the end, a location in the trees on a gentle slope looking onto open pasture was chosen and the project was ready to start.

THE DESIGN

The design was a simple gabled form resting on a cast-in-place concrete foundation. The students chose an exterior grade sign board for the siding and off-the-shelf corrugated galvanized metal as roofing. The interior was left unfinished with exposed framing lumber and plywood.

This was all that could realistically be managed in the time available and with the limited skills of the students. The Studio 804 that exists today was still many years of experience away. When the McCrea studio began, I had not given much thought to the overall organization of how a project would be collaboratively designed and built by students. I had not yet considered the management of their egos, personalities, desires and stamina that are now part of daily life working with Studio 804.

Judy loaned the students a four-wheel drive truck to use on the rough dirt road to access the property and they got started building. The Barber School was an emotional effort driven by the passions of that group of students to finish the project for Harris Stone. Not only did it offer the visual poetics of the historic stone walls, the steel roof, and the striking landscape but it was easy for the students to see it as a heroic mission, larger than themselves. In comparison, the McCrea studio was a down to the earth effort and the craft required was more functional than sculptural. Despite its simplicity, it was a more comprehensive building experience than the Barber School. Many of the issues are more complex and poor work is more glaring. They had to keep the weather out, build things square, make sure parts line up properly and they had to worry about issues like flashing details.

The initial wave of enthusiasm began to fade as the students were worn down by the grind of the manual labor and the unfamiliar problems they faced each day. They also had setbacks such as working in the mud during a typically wet spring in Kansas and at one point a storm knocked down their hard-earned progress - this added to the frustration and offered a lesson in bracing. The students had the best of intentions but soon a lot of my time was being spent trying to motivate them to be productive enough to finish the work on schedule. Eventually, workers from Rockhill and Associates had to help them finish.

THE MARVIN YARD CANOPY, 1997

University of Kansas Campus, Lawrence, Kansas

COMPAGNONS DU DEVOIR

After building the McCrea Studio I realized that if I was going to continue this type of work with students I had to plan and be ready to start on the first day of classes. I wanted to do more than routine construction work for a semester. I wanted the students to engage in a legitimate piece of architecture that would not only teach them the value of manual labor but would teach them about good design and how it can grow from an understanding of construction. I had always liked the ideas of the traditional French Guild the Compagnons du Devoir and the view expressed by their latter-day leader Jean Bernard. When my 1997 studio met, I hoped to live up to these aspirations:

> "From the beginning, man has been both manual and intellectual. Hand and mind have developed simultaneously without the former being the dregs of the other. The hand is not the vile instrument of the mind but its close associate, and generations pass down to one another, intermittent failures aside, the fruit of this union bestowed on man alone, the precious bequest slowly acquired that remains the just foundation of all education."[1]

AN OUTDOOR SHOP

Behind Marvin Hall, which houses the architecture department at the University of Kansas there was a neglected area of little used pavement that surrounded a utility shed. I felt this south facing space could be used to support the work being done by my studio and the practicum course I offered. The repercussion of architecture distancing itself from the act of construction was obvious to most and there was an increasing emphasis on opportunities for architecture students to work with their hands.

The design was to be a covered outdoor work space that could be used for larger mock-ups as well as activities better suited to the outdoors, such as welding. It also could function as a shelter for an outdoor classroom to be used during nice weather.

We approached the dean of the architecture school, John Gaunt with a design concept and mock-ups of the more complex connections for a steel and glass roof structure that would shelter the space. We asked if the school could fund the $10,000 needed for the work. Dean Gaunt supported the cause (as he did every year until his retirement in 2015) but could only offer to match whatever funds we could raise ourselves. This was good enough for us, so the students set out to find $5,000 in donations or material contributions. This was the beginning of the efforts that continue today to reach out to the building industry to support our mission with favorable pricing in exchange for the exposure that comes from being involved in such a unique educational program.

WORKING WITH THE UNIVERSITY

For this endeavor to happen it required more than my simply wanting to do it. I needed support from the upper administration to convince the university that it was an important educational mission. It had been nearly a century since architecture students had been expected to get dirty - let alone climb around on an open steel frame setting glass panels.

John's support was quickly tested. We were naïve to the ways of the university's building management bureaucracy. We were on a tight schedule to be finished by graduation and every day was important. Once we had the funds and materials on site we started building. The University of Kansas architect visited and asked the students what they were doing. They proudly told him. He and the university's Department of Construction Management (DCM), were not pleased and saw this as a serious break with protocol. They ordered that the work desist. John argued that the students were not required to seek the approvals and permits of a typical building project. He saw the effort as a form of research, which is a primary mission of all universities. Being as this was work by architecture students it was reasonable that the research would include building. It also helped the cause that the building included no services - it was simply a sculptural shelter and not really a building. The negotiations stopped us for a few days but after further conciliation everyone agreed to let the "research" continue.

DESIGNING WITH STUDENTS

The Barber School and McCrea studio had inherent limitations; this project was more of a blank slate to be filled. The students had been in design studios where they developed their own vision and felt complete ownership of their work. It was fortunate that this was a relatively simple structure and it served as a good trial run to teach students to work collaboratively on design rather than competing against one another to supply the vision.

THE DESIGN

What became known as the Building Technology Yard was a steel structure supporting a laminated glass roof. The shed roof was formed with triangular trusses fabricated with custom steel plate columns, hollow tube steel chords and round steel bar tension rods. The trusses were mounted to tapered concrete piers. Hollow tube steel purlins ran between the trusses and supported the 3/8" sheets of laminated glass that enclosed the roof and shed water. This project won a first-place award from the Association of Collegiate Schools of Architecture for student design work and also a design award from the steel industry. This recognition gave credence to what the class was doing, and the leverage needed to take the step of building a full house with the next year's studio.

1) Bernard, Jean, *Le Compagnonnage: Recontre de la jeunesse et de la tradition*. Paris, Presses, Universitaires de France, 1972, pp 593

B C
D E
F

B C D E *The Building Technology yard was used through 2013 when it was removed to build The Forum at Marvin Hall. It had served its purpose as the university had purchased a warehouse to function as a workshop for Studio 804 and many other classes that included building components in their educational efforts.*

F *It is likely that Studio 804 would have never gotten started without the complete support of Dean John Gaunt. John is shown here discussing progress of the canopy with some of the students.*

03

BECOMING STUDIO 804

By this time, students are signing up for a semester in my Arch 804 studio expecting a design/build experience. I start to plan for the semester and worked to create a more predictable strategy for finding worthwhile projects. During these years, we started building houses. After having done three simpler projects with minimal infrastructure this change made the day to day management of the class much more difficult. Those earlier projects were isolated activities that required minimal approvals and the involvement of few outside voices.

Now the students had to work with public entities, get building permits, address the concerns of the neighborhood and they had to coordinate their work with subcontractors and consultants. The first two projects were affordable infill projects done in Lawrence, Kansas with funding from the local governmental housing authorities using Housing and Neighborhood Block Grant funds. The others were done with a public affordable housing program whose mission was to enable members of the less advantaged community to enter the realm of home ownership.

933 PENNSYLVANIA HOUSE, 1998

East Lawrence Neighborhood, Lawrence, Kansas

AFFORDABLE HOUSING IN LAWRENCE

I needed to find a way to generate projects rather than chase funding possibilities every school year. In Lawrence in the late 1990s the housing market was booming. I thought there might be potential for students to build affordable housing to support the community. I knew the need existed and that most housing contractors were finding more profit building the large mansions that were feeding Lawrence's westward sprawl. I approached the Lawrence Housing Authority about supporting an effort by my design studio to build an affordable house in one of the established, older, and sometimes rundown neighborhoods near downtown and the University of Kansas campus. This was before the current trend to move back toward the core had fully gained momentum. There were still affordable vacant lots available and dilapidated properties mixed in with the well-kept historic homes, brick streets and the amenities of Lawrence.

The proposal was well received. With the support of Lawrence's Housing and Neighborhood Development office and a community development block grant The Lawrence Housing Authority made available the resources for us to build a house in the East Lawrence Neighborhood within walking distance of downtown. Later, we would learn that there was a lack of clear communication about design goals but when the project began everyone felt it was serving their purpose.

Our building site had belonged to the local activist Shelly Miller. She had bought several parcels of land in East Lawrence to protect them from commercial developers who were knocking down houses in the older neighborhoods and replacing them with poorly built apartments. When she died, a charitable trust was formed in her name and they decided to make this piece of property available to us. They intended to support efforts to build single family housing that would be affordable for people with low to moderate incomes.

DESIGN MANAGEMENT

Up to this project the design process with the students had been straightforward. The Marvin Yard Canopy for example had been simple in its program and the students did not have any experience with the building type. They had few preconceived notions, so we focused on learning how to manipulate the steel and concrete details. It was easy for me steer them toward a unique but manageable solution. Everyone has preconceived notions about what a house should be. Combine this with the autonomous way most students design in their classroom studios and 933 Pennsylvania became a learning experience for me as well as the students. It required more finesse to develop an effective design process that led to a building that met the design standards I set for myself and the program.

I also had to learn to schedule a project built exclusively with students, most of whom had little or no experience building and who expected to be done by graduation. I knew I would have to be on site much of the time to assure progress. I also was still engaged in day to day work of Rockhill and Associates. I started the semester anxious to get this house out of the ground as soon as possible. I ended up learning that if we take a little more time during design development the final product will benefit and the construction process simpler and faster. This does not mean I am not proud of the work, or the students. They did an absurd amount work in a very short time and none of us really knew what we are getting into when we started.

THE DESIGN

The house was designed to work with the sloping site by stepping the interior spaces around a wet core that contains the bathrooms and laundry. The three stories hold three-bedrooms and three bathrooms in a deceptively small gabled volume. The lowest floor opens to the backyard and the driveway where the occupants can park off the alley. Inside, is a mudroom with access to storage, a small utility bathroom and the mechanical room. Up a short set of stairs on the south side of the wet core is a two-story living room with an open kitchen. From there, stairs on the north side of the wet core lead to a bedroom/office at the back of the house. The front of the living room is wrapped by an open staircase that leads to the second floor where there are two-bedrooms, one on each side of the bathroom and a laundry room housed at the top of the wet core.

DO-IT-YOURSELF

As is a trademark of Studio 804's do-it-yourself approach, we custom built many of the architectural components for the house. Often using reclaimed materials. The students fabricated their own kitchen and storage cabinets, stair railings and installed a salvaged tongue and groove oak floors that had been removed from an old Veterans of Foreign Wars (VFW) hall. We used material salvaged from a demolished industrial facility to weld the steel frames that make up the entry deck and its roof.

We made our own light fixtures which led to some early lessons about how far custom fabrication will be allowed to extend. The city inspector would not pass our initial effort since the fixture was not UL rated. We had to redesign our fixture to act as a shroud around an existing UL rated unit.

WORKING IN LAWRENCE

As the project started to take shape and people began to see what it was going to look like there was a backlash from some in the neighborhood. This resistance found its way to the door of the Housing Authority and its workers responding by saying we

A *As we did on the McCrea studio the exterior is clad with Crezon, a sign painter's board that is commonly used for highway signage. This makes for a tightly skinned envelope topped by a shallow gabled roof with deep eaves. The windows are trimmed with trex, a synthetic wood made from recycled content and set to protrude from the smooth surface to become objects on the walls.*

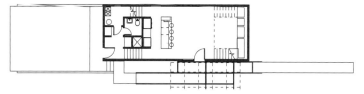

Lower Floor Plan

First Floor Plan

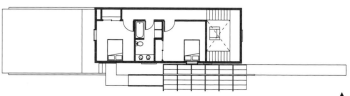

Second Floor Plan

N

B C
—————
   D

B *We extensively salvaged materials. This was before the secondary markets for used materials became so lucrative. We began to nurture contacts with demolition contractors who would alert us if there were any useful materials to be removed before a building's demolition. In this case an old VFW hall had oak flooring that we removed and then installed in the house. We would not have been able to afford a new wood floor of this quality.*

had misled them. Working through these types of roadblocks - and learning how to avoid them - with good, open communication has proven to a valuable part of the Studio 804 education.

It was nothing new to me as Rockhill and Associates had extensive experience with Lawrence's unique combination of progressive activism and Midwest conservatism. The town is a bohemian oasis that was founded by abolitionists and it still represents this inclusive view of the American culture. There is strong support for individual dignity and human rights and a focus on the type of development that supports these views such as access to affordable, accessible and sustainable housing. This activism has been mostly positive for Lawrence

with a primary example being the communities aggressive resistance to a cornfield mall like the ones that decimated the downtown of many Midwest cities in the 1970s and 80s. That said, at times this activism reaches into architectural aesthetics in restrictive ways that can make modern design difficult. There is widespread preference for a contextual historicism when working on new structures in the old neighborhoods. New work is expected to be subservient to the old and should be designed with this in mind. In the years since, 933 Pennsylvania has been used as an example of what not to do when building in the East Lawrence Neighborhood. This created a tense situation when we started planning for our next house and were looking at property only a couple of blocks away.

1144 PENNSYLVANIA HOUSE, 1999

East Lawrence Neighborhood, Lawrence, Kansas

THE SITE

Both I and the Lawrence Housing Authority learned lessons while building the house at 933 Pennsylvania. I had a better idea of what to expect from the students and knew what concerns were likely to be voiced by the community. The housing authority - though they expected and preferred a more conventional design - were happy 933 Pennsylvania was completed on schedule, on budget and was occupied by satisfied owners. Both of us were willing to work together again. We found a piece of property with a long ignored derelict house that was beyond repair. The city removed the house and with the support of community development block grant funds we started.

For this house, more time was allotted for perfecting the design and making sure all the students, as well as myself, were devoted to the effort before we broke ground. I encouraged a building form and details that were clearly modern but found their inspiration in the history of vernacular architecture in the region and the character of the neighborhood. The East Lawrence neighborhood is a rich blend of architectural styles and degrees of sophistication. It ranges from small civil war era hovels to large Victorians of the late 19th century that would have housed leaders in the community. There are wood framed houses, brick and stone masonry buildings and all sorts of quirky adaptations and outbuildings that have arisen through the years. There is no overriding aesthetic, but we did work to conform to the scale, orientation and setbacks of the environs. We settled on a long,

$$\frac{\quad B \quad}{A \quad C \; D}$$

A *When starting the project at 933 Pennsylvania Street we submitted for a building permit. The submittal had to have a name on it. One of the students suggested Studio 804, being as the design studio was ARCH 804. By the time we submitted for this building permit it was the name of the program.*

D *When it came time to sell the house the city ended up with so many applicants that they held a lottery of all the qualified buyers. The buyers had to be of low or moderate income and they had to be a couple or family. The winner of the lottery was a single mother with young children. She is shown here with the mayor of Lawrence at the time.*

narrow gabled form that sat comfortably on its corner lot, its proportions like many of the houses nearby while also offering the opportunity to take advantage of the unencumbered southern exposure. We responded to the most often voiced concern about 933 Pennsylvania and included a front porch along the primary street elevation.

THE DESIGN

The most distinct characteristic of the 1350 square-foot, three-bedroom house is the two-story custom built, steel framed, polycarbonate glazed, light box and ventilation chimney on the south elevation. It floods the two-story space at the heart of the house with indirect daylight. At night, it is a glowing lantern when viewed from the street. At the base of the box are four operable windows that bring in fresh air which is vented through windows on the second floor. The framing of the house was kept relatively simple so the students could spend significant design time working out the exposed steel detailing and the glazing for this feature. It, along with the custom welded porch awnings and exposed eaves create the delicate balance between the modern and the vernacular that we were trying to achieve.

The first floor is fully accessible. A barrier free walkway leads to the south door from the off-street parking provided at the back of the site. Inside is a two-story living room which is flooded with diffuse sunlight. It is open to the kitchen toward the front of the house and a short hallway leads to a bedroom tucked behind the bathroom and laundry. A set of exposed stairs wrap the living room and end at a second-floor bridge open to the living room below and the light box's glazed wall. To the back of the house from the bridge is a bathroom and the master bedroom. At the front of the bridge is a room isolated from the rest of the house that can serve as a bedroom, guest room or study.

RAINSCREEN

The house's distinct siding is a low maintenance rainscreen. This is the first of many rainscreens Studio 804 has done. Rainscreens were developed in Norway to help alleviate the damage done to traditionally detailed siding by the incessant moisture which would get trapped in the wall assembly and eventually result in mildew and decay. A rainscreen is designed to allow the assembly to breath. The finish siding is held off the moisture barrier and detailed to vent air at the top and bottom. On the precious sunny days that do occur the sun heats the siding which heats the air behind. The warmed air rises and is released at the top which pulls cooler dry air in from below and creates a constant flow of air to dry the moisture that has collected.

There are other sustainable advantages to a rainscreen. The siding shades the moisture barrier meaning the heat of the sun does not reach the exterior of the insulated wall assembly.

Also, since the siding does not have to be the moisture barrier it opens many options. Just about any material that does not simply rot if left exposed becomes a potential siding. Materials that expand and contract or even ones that warp and crack have potential use if fastened correctly.

The technology of the moisture barrier was rudimentary in 1999 but it was still a significant step in creating a long lasting, healthy and sustainable wall assembly. The weather barriers are now much more sophisticated in their installation as well as the way they manage moisture vs. vapor. They also are better equipped to withstand the sun's UV rays if portions are consistently exposed. Learning about these new building strategies is part of being a student in Studio 804. First, we research these products and see if they are applicable to our work. If so, we reach out to the industry representatives and see if they are interested in working with us. Quite often this results in favorable pricing and our work gives their new products wide exposure as our work was being published and winning design awards.

At 1144 Pennsylvania, the moisture barrier was a peel and stick ice and water shield. Over it we ran vertical sleepers on to which we fastened the horizontally run cement fiber board slats, leaving an air gap between each. This resulted in a siding that blends in with the typical horizontal clapboards of the neighborhood but also is reminiscent of the spaced siding one would see on a vernacular corn crib. Once again, we balanced the techniques of the region and the context of the neighborhood. The Lawrence Housing Authority was concerned about the use of this relatively untested technology being used on a house they were funding. Before we were permitted to purchase the materials, we had to agree that we would resolve any problems related to the rainscreen - including the supposedly inevitable mud dauber, wasp and bird nests that would fill the voids we were creating. This is a question we consistently had to address about rainscreens as we continued to use them. It has not been a problem for this house or any of the other rainscreens on which we have worked.

This was not the only problem related to the siding. We had noted on the approved drawings that the house would be painted yellow. Apparently, this was assumed to be a gentler, antique Victorian yellow rather than the DeWalt yellow we chose. The housing authority insisted that we paint it another color. This dispute lasted for weeks until the East Lawrence Neighborhood Association who had become supporters of our work intervened and said they were pleased with the color. Since they spoke for those the city felt they were protecting they relented and allowed the house to remain the yellow that it still is today.

MONEY FLOW
While working with The Lawrence Housing Authority we were given a budget, but we had no access to the money. This inconvenience was exacerbated by the fact that every single purchase, every nut and bolt, had to be released with a purchase order which required students to first go to city hall to obtain the PO number and then go and buy the item. This drove the poor city employee who issued the orders as well as my students to near madness.

This type of arrangement did not work then, nor would it work today for a Studio 804 project. For most low-income housing, there is very little custom work. The builders adapt the design to the site with as little variation as possible and nearly every purchase order could be placed before the construction even starts. They can operate this way with little inconvenience. For a Studio 804 project, no matter the budget, we design on the go. Our schedule makes it impossible to do otherwise. I also like the significant learning opportunities presented by the improvisational efforts to solve critical problems immediately. We do what is required to get a building permit and feel confident about the overall costs, but many design features are addressed when they must be. We solve issues by hand, on the site during construction, or for the more complicated problems we build mock-ups, studying options until we have an acceptable result. This happens nearly every day and it leads to regular runs to the store for the immediate materials need. Having to submit paper work every time we need a fastener was crippling our process and I felt was limiting our potential. This was just one of a list of concerns that had to be addressed if I was going to continue to do this annually.

1144 PENNSYLVANIA HOUSE, 1999

First Floor Plan

N

Second Floor Plan

216 ALABAMA HOUSE, 2000

The Pinckney Neighborhood, Lawrence, Kansas

BECOMING A CORPORATION

At the turn of the century the work of Studio 804 was gaining respect in both professional and educational circles. It was part of the architectural curriculum at the University of Kansas and it was being used in promotional material to recruit students. If the program was going to continue to grow it needed to be more legitimate than the ad hoc effort it had been thus far. My colleague at the university, Kent Spreckelmeyer suggested that we were held in high enough regard that it would be appropriate to seek becoming a not for profit corporation.

I had received minimal support from the university and was not really seeking more. I wanted to answer to as few people as possible and if the university's exposure to liability were to increase so would their input. That said, I could not comfortably continue as I had been. Studio 804 had been working under the umbrella of my Rockhill and Associates insurance for liability, worker compensation and builder's risk as well as - in name only - the General Contractor for our license with the city. It seemed unnecessary to put my business in jeopardy, but it was admittedly convenient. With Kent's enormous help I resolved these issues in a manner that still functions with only minimal changes today. By the end of the project at 216 Alabama we were a not for profit 501(c)3 corporation - Studio 804 Inc. We had a board of directors and an affiliated agreement laying out the responsibilities and liabilities between us and the University of Kansas. Although my feelings were slightly hurt at the time the way we resolved the affiliation agreement with the University was the best thing that ever happened despite my not realizing it at the time. We were now a legitimate business entity that could negotiate with community and industrial representatives without apology and we were mostly free of University involvement in our day to day operation.

Kent, not only believed in the value building experience brought to an architect's education but he was also willing to help me organize the concept in the school's curriculum - starting with his own course in management. He offered to use his fall semester class as a venue for the students to do the leg work necessary to identify a project for my spring semester. They worked with Kent to secure funding, develop client user relations, study zoning and codes, develop neighborhood connections, learn about ADA accessibility and more. I could then hit the ground running when the students joined me in January and be on site as soon as possible.

Kent's devotion and tenacity in helping me build the foundation for Studio 804 and shaping it into viable program and business cannot be over stated. I am indebted to him for his vision and support. Many of the steps we took at that time remain in place today and prepared us well to continue to grow.

TENANTS TO HOMEOWNERS

The Lawrence Housing Authority had been supportive and helped get us up and running but they had had enough of our intransigence by the end of the second house so we went in search of a new partner to fund our work. 216 Alabama was the first house we did with Tenants to Homeowners (now the Lawrence Community Housing Trust), a not for profit organization devoted to providing affordable housing for buyers with low to moderate income. They offer a stock of renovated or newly constructed houses at subsidized sale prices. In exchange for this value, the buyers agree that when they elect to re-sell, they will re-sell to another income-eligible buyer at a formula price that allows buyers to earn a fair amount of equity, while keeping the home affordable. They shared Studio 804's interest in innovative, accessible and affordable design and offered to give us a site and fund our construction.

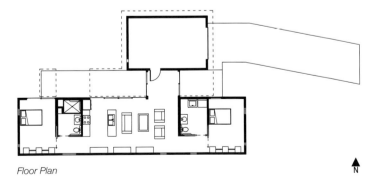

Floor Plan

N

A
—
B

A B *The exterior siding is Okoume, a marine grade plywood that was harvested in Gabon. It is typically used in boat building and when properly treated has a high UV resistance.*

C D
—————
   E

Universal design guidelines go well beyond simple wheelchair accessibility. It is a broad-spectrum plan to produce buildings that are inherently accessible to everyone. The design considers the way reduced senses or arthritis or diabetes might change the way we interact with a house. The students wanted to turn the elimination of barriers into a design asset that defined the use and aesthetics of the house.

The resulting house is a series of Okoume clad boxes on a foundation that creates level plane above the site that slopes away from the street. The driveway acts as an entry ramp that dies flush into the west end of the deck. This deck plane extends the length of the house, only broken by the transparent box of the breezeway that acts as an entry and connects the box of the house and to the box of the garage. The breezeway is the heart of circulation through the house. Sliding glass doors are used to eliminate the difficulty of maneuvering around the swing of hinged doors. The primary residence is a long rectangular box with an open plan. Bedrooms are located at each end screened from the living areas by translucent boxes that house the bathrooms, laundry and mechanical spaces. These boxes are custom steel frames clad with two layers of polycarbonate. The plumbing and fixtures become ghostly shadows when the lights are turned on while the occupants are indistinct formless shadows. The house opens to the outdoor deck through the length of the south elevation. The sculptural custom fabricated steel awnings not only shelter the deck but have been calculated to promote passive heating and cooling by shading the summer sun from entering the house while allowing the low winter sun to penetrate the space.

The cabinetry throughout is custom made with birch plywood. Since the north wall had limited openings - only what was needed for cross ventilation - we used this wall for a continuous run of storage units of different sizes and depths.

In addition to passive techniques we continued to explore the possibilities of salvaged materials and those made with recycled and rapidly renewable content. The roof's aluminum sheet shingles are industrial waste, the living room floors are bamboo and the bathroom floors recycled rubber tires.

Compared to the house before it and the one after I did not feel that we reached the level of refinement we might have. As has been the case each year I am still indebted to the students for the effort and enthusiasm they put into these projects, but with hindsight I could see where this project became more complicated than it needed to be. There were too many isolated ideas, each one well executed but they did not jell into a solid composition. It was another chapter in the delicate process of trying to meld the ideas of a group of students of varying backgrounds, personalities and energy into a cohesive group all pulling the rope in the same direction. I had not yet learned to do this every year.

PINCKNEY NEIGHBORHOOD

216 Alabama is in the Pinckney neighborhood which is another older neighborhood, but it is further from downtown and the University than East Lawrence and is often lost in the discussions about Lawrence's neighborhoods. It has suffered from a lack of the sidewalks and alleys found in the other neighborhoods and it has been chopped up by development. Significant portions have gone through re-zoning several times as the area shifted from primarily residential, to commercial and then medical. The site is one block from the Lawrence Memorial Hospital and is adjacent to one of the many health related facilities that are nearby and help support the hospital. Despite this there are still many positives to the neighborhood as some of the oldest historic houses and historic blocks in Lawrence are here and parts of it have a rural quality even though it is firmly in the middle of town.

UNIVERSAL AND ACCESSIBLE DESIGN

The previous houses had been accessible but were still two-story structures. For this 1200 square-foot two-bedroom house the students wanted to further the stated mission of Tenants to Homeowners by making the entire house accessible and universally designed.

D E *The walls of the bathrooms are sheathed with extruded polycarbonate panels that are typically used in greenhouse construction.*

RANDOM ROAD HOUSE, 2001

Brook Creek Neighborhood, Lawrence, Kansas

CURRICULUM

At this time, students in Studio 804 had to do this very demanding work while taking other courses. This meant they would come and go through the day as their schedules would fluctuate with the demands of these other classes. It made it hard to plan the on-site tasks and keep the project on schedule. I never knew how many people would be on site at any given time. I wanted to continue building more demanding houses, so I began to explore options with other faculty members and the architecture program about dedicating time exclusively to Studio 804. I was fortunate, I had the almost unanimous support of the faculty - they saw that the program was evolving into something of great value and were willing to put aside their own convenience to help me. Again, with the help of Kent and John, I was able to formalize Studio 804's niche in the architecture curriculum as the final design studio for graduate students. Classes that in the past would have conflicted with our work were moved to a different semester or if that was impossible they were at least moved to the evenings to free up the precious daytime hours.

Studio 804, although not a required studio was now a comprehensive building experience meaning there was overlap with some courses. We approached those who taught professional practices and programming to see if we were covering the subject listed on their syllabus. It was apparent that our work, in a very real context, overlapped and exceeded the course expectations that were

being met in the classroom. Using the syllabi of these courses the students documented all relevant experience and were, in the end, given credit for the courses. I remain thankful to the faculty who taught these classes for agreeing to these changes and helping Studio 804 reach its potential.

MORTGAGES

I was interested in exploring more fundamentally creative solutions for the affordable housing market. Ones that would result in smaller, efficient houses that used space well. But, the way properties are sold, and the way banks work makes this difficult. I was not operating with my own money and could not risk the houses remaining unsold. We had to work around the traditional three-bedroom layout with a garage. It did not seem to me that a garage was the most important amenity for those on a limited income, a nice carport would suffice. But, even this break from the norm is difficult if the buyer requires a mortgage loan - which for these houses were sure to be the case. Banks loan to the properties appraised value. Upping the appraised value of a house remains a challenge for our work even today, but it was much more acute during these years. We were building houses specifically for low and moderate income families that had to meet specific requirements set by the Lawrence Housing Authority or Tenants to Homeowners for assistance. If the buyers had the money on hand to purchase the house with cash it was not likely they would qualify. Eventually, the transaction was going to hinge on the appraised value and the value of homes seen as comparable. Appraisals are formatted in such a way that they remove the subjective evaluation of the appraiser from the process. The value is set by measurables like the overall square-footage and the number of bedrooms and bathrooms. There is also value in quantifiable amenities like a basement, a garage, and outdoor decks. The quality of the construction, the use of sustainable materials and the reduction of energy consumption are not part of the formula. Certainly, good design cannot be part of the equation since there is not a universal consensus of how it is defined.

I felt then, as I do now, that good modern design creates houses that stand out in a market full of variations on the same thing. There would be few comparables, thus less competition for the buyers to use in negotiations. Studio 804 has proven this true several times over the years. But, it is a two-sided coin. The appraised value used by the banks is also based on comparables – for how much have similar houses in similar markets sold. Even while building the relatively conservative house during these early years there were no direct comparables for what we were doing. Our work would be equated to other houses of the same size being built in the older neighborhoods but too much lesser standards. We would end up doing research in other similar communities trying to find modern houses of similar size and prove that design had value, but it never helped much in the end.

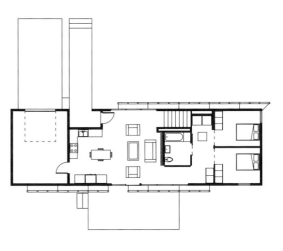

Ground Floor Plan

N

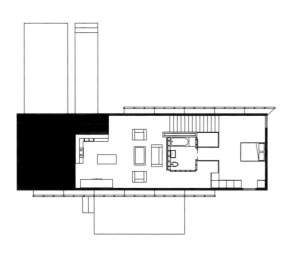

Upper Floor Plan

A   D
_____
B C   E F G H

A *All the exterior decks are kept minimal by assuring they never reach heights that would require a railing and by welding custom steel frames that hide the connections to the ground allowing the decks to appear to float in the air.*

B C *The spacing and angle of the redwood slats that had once visually shielded the cooling tower in Coffeyville, Kansas were appropriately spaced to use for seasonal sun control. All we had to do was adapt the notched verticals to our support brackets and we were able to re-insert the louvres in the original vertical boards.*

D G *We embraced the past of the salvaged floor boards and allowed the paint that once created the markings on a court for basketball and volleyball to create a random, abstract pattern through the house.*

H *The two-story bathroom core is made with custom welded steel frames clad with two layers of polycarbonate panels to create a lantern that can be used to softly light the main volume.*

THE SITE

The site on Random Road was different from the others we had worked on. It was the remnant of a large subdivision laid out by land planners as Lawrence spread south. It was not my favorite location as it was further from downtown and surrounded by relatively uninspired mid-twentieth century houses when compared to the rich setting of the older neighborhoods. The attractive part of it for me, and ironically probably the reason it was still available, was that it was an odd shaped site, isolated from view and adjacent to the original barnyard, barn and silo of the farm that once occupied the land. Apparently, no one knew what to do with this property, so it fell to us. It was a good fit. I liked the extra room, appreciated the existing structures and it offered the open southern exposure we coveted for passive heating and cooling strategies.

THE DESIGN

This three-bedroom, 1500 square-foot structure is another study in full ADA accessibility, universal design and sustainability. The open living room and kitchen along with two-bedrooms are located on the barrier free First Floor. The third bedroom is in a loft space on the second floor and is accessed by a set of stairs wide enough to accommodate a chair lift. The loft includes a bathroom, so it can be used as a master bedroom suite, an office or as accommodations for a care giver.

With each project, we tried to find new and exciting ways to use salvaged materials. This project has an exceptional example. Since we were taking advantage of the southern exposure we needed to devise louvres or an awning to control the depth of the sun's penetration into the house. Fortunately, we received word of a redwood clad cooling tower that was slated for demolition in Coffeyville, Kansas and we were given permission to remove this treasure of beautiful wood. It included dimension lumber as well as hundreds of 1/2" x 6" x 36" slats. They had been used to screen the cooling towers and now we were using them to control the sun. We fabricated steel brackets that extend from the steel rainscreen and support the vertical redwood, clear all-heart dimension lumber that was already notched to receive the louvres.

The interior flooring is maple tongue and groove gymnasium flooring we removed from a facility in north Kansas City that had been damaged by a roof leak. We mobilized and in a few hours had removed hundreds of square feet of hard wood maple flooring. It was nearly new and most of it had not been damaged by the water. We used what we needed at Random Road and stored the rest for future projects.

SIDING

We planned to do another rainscreen. When we were exploring options for the siding we wanted a material that would be as low maintenance as possible and would accentuate the redwood as well as the salvaged aluminum we used for trim details. We settled on panels of weathering steel. It was a good choice and helped to create what was the first of Studio 804s relatively minimal designs. This house more than any of the others is a prelude to where the program heads architecturally. I was learning to better work with the students and their ambitions.

ATHERTON COURT HOUSE, 2003

Brook Creek Neighborhood, Lawrence, Kansas

THE SITE

This project was even further afield in the Brook Creek neighborhood. Property values were skyrocketing close to town and affordable housing was being pushed to the perimeter. In this case, we were a fish out of water, surrounded by Habitat for Humanity houses which were designed in the vocabulary of the American suburbs. I had a sense that we were out of sync with the community we were working to serve. Not only did the banks prefer more conventional design but I increasingly felt that those buying the houses would have preferred a more conventional solution. I was convinced there was a market for our work as we envisioned it - where it would be appreciated for more than simply being affordable and available. When this house was finished, I felt it was time to find a new way to reach this market.

THE DESIGN

With hindsight, I feel we over reached on this house. In comparison to the refined simplicity of the house at Random Road this design was trying too hard and was too dependent upon the engagement of the occupant to keep it looking as pristine as we imagined. As is always the case I remain inspired by the energy and creativity the students bring to the program and this was a good group. My loss of enthusiasm for this project in no way reflects on their effort or skills.

We once again designed a house to be as accessible, affordable and sustainable as possible. Care was taken to make sure all features were barrier free and meet the universal design standards. The house is composed of two forms with the kitchen acting as a hinge between. The volume to the south holds the living room and two-bedrooms, one to each side of a bathroom. The south wall is extensively glazed and lined with water tubes that act as mass to absorb the sun's heat and release it into the space at night. We used cellular insulated shades with the industry standard insulated "super glass" units to cut down on heat loss by offering wall like R-values. The north wall is lined with custom built storage units and supports just the windows needed to promote cross ventilation.

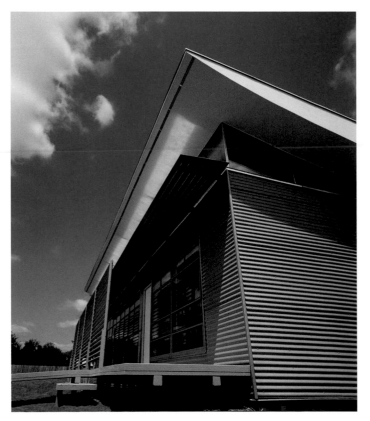

Floor Plan

A	C
B	D E

A *As property values close to downtown Lawrence increased the affordable housing efforts were pushed outward and the work of Studio 804 was not a good fit on car-oriented streets with their prominent garage doors.*

D *To create the dramatic forms that compose this house the students had to work creatively with a composite structure of engineered lumber and beams as well as steel.*

E *Hovering above all the rooms in the house is the cloud like roof form that shapes the light entering the house. The belly like ceiling being a curved form that the students built with hundreds of 2 x 4s, leftover from our concrete foundation formwork. They extend from the rafters and support the painted drywall.*

This was our first time to use white single ply membrane roofing. It was relatively new to the market at the time. It offered a light reflective alternative to the standard black membranes and bitumen roofing that absorbed heat and contributed to the creation of urban heat islands.

In the volume to the north of the kitchen is the garage that opens to the back of the house. Being on a corner lot we could hide the garage door and avoid the typical garage centric street elevation so typical to the suburbs and the surrounding houses. Between the kitchen and the garage is a flexible space with a bathroom that like the house on Random Road, can serve as a third bedroom, an office or accommodate a care giver or independent family member.

THE MOVE TO KANSAS CITY
It did not appear I was going to be able to easily do the type of work I wanted to do in Lawrence much longer. Neighborhoods in Lawrence are relatively healthy and no matter how downtrodden a block or two might appear the proximity to downtown Lawrence and the University of Kansas sets a floor for property values in the worst of times. At the turn of the century these properties were booming in value. Houses and property were worth two or three times what they had been in 1990. This

meant there were few, if any, empty, affordable lots, especially compared to most larger cities where vacancy was epidemic. Also, Lawrence is a town with a rich pre civil-war history and has an active preservation community. It is peppered with registered historic properties as well as several registered districts. This means a significant percentage of the properties in established neighborhoods require a Historic Resources Commission review. These reviews take valuable time making it difficult to do houses within the Studio 804 framework.

In Kansas City, Kansas, where we would end up working for the next four years, we could find property that was free or nearly free and put our resources into the architecture. Also, most of the neighborhoods and affordable housing authorities were so hungry for development they were not interested in judging the appearance of our work or its coherence to housing orthodoxy. In this climate, we found we could reach out to young, aspiring urbanites who were not deterred by the school district or worried about the curb appeal of their neighbor's houses. They were a market that did not really exist in a college town. They saw themselves as urban pioneers who appreciated the rich potential of living amongst a diverse population and, despite having limited funds, dreamed of living in a house like the ones they saw in Dwell magazine.

04

INFRASTRUCTURE

When Studio 804 began, each year was its own adventure. There was no organizational carry over from year to year. We had no money we could call our own, we worked under my business' insurance and all the equipment and tools were stored in my barn and outbuildings. Each time we broke ground I had faith that things would work out in the end. After a few projects, I realized I would have to legitimize the process if it were to continue - not only for liability reasons but also to allow the program to reach its full potential as an educational model.

To do this, Studio 804 became a not-for-profit 501(c)3 corporation. Now we have a board of directors, a bookkeeper, the insurance required to operate as architects and contractors and there is an affiliated agreement laying out the responsibilities and liabilities between Studio 804 and the University of Kansas. Even after setting all of this up we remained vagabond for many years moving from warehouse to warehouse until we finally settled in our current home in a university owned facility,

THE YEARLY OPERATION
OF STUDIO 804

An East Hills Business Park Warehouse, Lawrence, Kansas

STUDENTS

Each year, between 15 to 20 students sign up for Studio 804.
It started as a one semester offering for graduate students
and was taken in addition to the rest of their courses. When we
started building houses I explored ways to lessen these demands.
It was hard to schedule work on a job site when students were
leaving for class in the middle of a task. With the cooperation
of the administration and a supportive faculty I was able to first
reduce, and then gradually eliminate this conflict. We started by
moving required courses to different semesters or offering them
in the evening. We also found ways to credit the student for
courses where the syllabus overlapped with what we were doing.

By the early 2000's Studio 804 was becoming a nationally recognized program, this coincided with the School of Architecture and
Design efforts to develop new track guidelines for its master's
program. I was interested in extending Studio 804 to an entire
school year, feeling there was potential for the program to offer
even more than it was at the time. The University saw value that
went beyond my self-interests. The master's track for architecture was changed so that students finish all but studio offerings
entering their final year. This not only accommodated my goals - I
now had nearly nine unencumbered months to work with the students - but it also opened many other educational avenues at the
University of Kansas. Soon there was a studio offering in Paris,
France, a professional internship at a design firm in Kansas City
and it was during this time that Architecture of Health and Well-
ness got its start. It has become a well-respected program that
is bringing people to Kansas to study health care architecture.

At the Barber School, and for a few years afterwards, I was
primarily working with students who were already enrolled at the
University of Kansas. My studio was the one they happened to
take. Eventually students were coming to Kansas planning to
complete their master's degree by working on a Studio 804 project. Other faculty and advisors were aware of our work and started steering promising candidates our direction. I now work with
aspiring architects from all over world of varying backgrounds
and life experiences brought together in Kansas, in the middle of
flyover America, starting in the heat of August but with winter on
its way. They are required to work together as a team and overcome significant challenges and achieve very demanding goals.

NOT-FOR-PROFIT

After building the first couple of houses I realized I would need
a more legitimate platform from which to operate. We had
started working on projects that required building permits and
inspections, that had to wind their way through neighborhood
associations and historic resources boards and we had started

approaching material suppliers and manufacturers to donate or discount their products to help us explore unique design solutions. We were also reaching out to numerous community and governmental organizations to help us create and fund projects. These people needed assurances as to what they were getting themselves into if they chose to work with us. Studio 804 had to clearly be more than weekenders knocking out a small project between classes.

When building the 216 Alabama Street House in 2000 the not-for-profit 501(c)3 Studio 804 Inc. was formed. We also formalized the relationship with the University. Studio 804 is now a non-controlled affiliated corporation with an affiliation agreement laying out the responsibilities and liabilities between us and the University of Kansas.

The internet was not yet part of my daily practice at that time, nor was it yet the internet we now know. Today, one can go on-line and in minutes be set up as 501(c)3. I had to have a lawyer submit the required paper work to get us running.

Even though it takes little effort to become a not-for-profit corporation it does necessitate regular and thoughtful bookkeeping to retain the status. We must file tax statements with the State of Kansas as well as the federal government each year and I am required to have a board of directors who meet with some regularity. It is composed of students, professionals and several colleagues, all of whom are very supportive of the program, several of whom remain on the board nearly 20 years since its inception. These meetings are, for the most part, perfunctory as I simply keep everyone up to date about where we stand. They do require me to slow down and reflect on the program and the input of the board members often brings a fresh perspective to the issues I am facing.

BOOKKEEPING

I think it is safe to say few students have balanced a check book when they join Studio 804 and that very few are experienced at keeping paperwork and documenting their purchases and worrying about things such as taxes. It is realistic to assume that today's student will have never even written a check and the idea of financial responsibility is checking their balance on their smartphone. On our projects, they learn that every piece of paper and every receipt and e-mail that relates to the purchase or donation of a product or service is vital. Each must be kept or saved and properly filed. The students facilitate hundreds of purchases and agreements, some large, many small and they occur regularly. Every check that is written must have an invoice attached and the records must be clear and organized for the reports that will be filed later. This is a valuable experience for the students. They are required to learn a process, respect the steps, and take responsibility for their actions.

Every year a student is assigned - or volunteers to be - the bookkeeper for the class. He or she writes all the checks as needed for Studio 804 and brings them to me to sign and then distributes them as required. This student bookkeeper makes sure all the bills are paid before the due dates and all reimbursements are handled professionally and quickly. I let them

know they hold the reputation of Studio 804 in their hands and not only does this impact their class but the ones that come later. It is not a glamorous role to accept when we are dividing responsibilities. I doubt any architecture student pictures themselves being a bookkeeper when they sign up for Studio 804, but this is one of the most impactful roles in the smooth operation of a project. The students who did it well have earned a special place in my memory.

The student bookkeeper enters all the information on a simple spread sheet where it can be quickly accessed and reviewed. For many years, it was just me and the student who kept this in order and passed the information from class to class. In recent years as the projects have become larger and more complicated I have had to make changes to satisfy institutional concerns from the University. The string of educational buildings required Rockhill and Associates to act as the Architect of Record and stamp all the drawings. This naturally increased the amount of time dedicated to Studio 804 by my Rockhill and Associates staff. I used Studio 804 funds to reimburse Rockhill and Associates for the time. I was transparent in all these transactions, but it caused stress for some at the University who are sensitive to the even the appearance of a conflict of interest. To alleviate these concerns, I now have an independent professional bookkeeper who reviews the work and signs all checks between Studio 804 and Rockhill and Associates. To accommodate this extra set of eyes and the growing complexity of the work we started also using Intuit's QuickBooks to store and organize our records even though I still require the quick and easy to read spread sheet be kept updated to summarize the work.

The bookkeeping demands of the not-for-profit corporation do have side benefits for Studio 804 since we are always working to achieve LEED Platinum status as well as other sustainable certifications. Since we already are required to document every purchase and service we are well positioned for the demanding paperwork required for LEED or Passive House US (PHIUS) certification as these programs require extensive documentation of the products used in the construction of the building.

INSURANCE

In many municipalities, including our own, contractors are expected to prove they have the required insurance to get a building permit. For the first couple of projects I did this under the umbrella of my Rockhill and Associates policies. Like many other aspects of the evolution of Studio 804 this became more tenuous as the projects became more complicated and more people and agencies became involved. In the years since, Studio 804 Inc. has developed the type of insurance portfolio that is necessary to function as a full-scale design/build firm - University affiliated or not.

COVERAGES

a) Studio 804 carries commercial liability insurance to protect the program against any occurrences stipulated in the policy selected. There is a broad menu from which to select coverages and each are tied to a cost. We get by with what we think

we need but it does come at a hefty price although one I advise everyone to have before taking on any exposure with students.

b) Studio 804 carries builder's risk insurance to cover the materials and equipment being used on the project in case of theft or damage. You cannot purchase home owner's insurance until there is a finished home to insure so this covers the same type of damages during construction.

c) Studio 804 carries director's Insurance which assure those on the corporation's board of directors that they are protected from liability or legal fees in relation to the work of Studio 804 and cannot be personally sued. This must be renewed each year and the information shared with the board members.

d) Errors and Omissions (E&O) insurance is carried by Rockhill and Associates which covers Studio 804 when a project requires an architect's stamp and Rockhill and Associates acts as the Architect of Record. This insurance protects Studio 804 and Rockhill and Associates against being sued for a failure to deliver the agreed upon services. The yearly E&O costs are determined by the yearly Rockhill and Associates receipts. Since Rockhill and Associates is a relatively small firm it is easy to isolate the added insurance costs associated with the Studio 804 work, Studio 804, through the independent bookkeeper, reimburses Rockhill and Associates for the costs related to Studio 804's undertakings.

e) Each student is required to have a proof of health insurance. Some are covered by their parents, others have paid for insurance sponsored by the University of Kansas. Still others have worked with a local private insurer to purchase a policy to protect them in case of an injury related to the job site.

f) Despite Studio 804 having no paid employees I still prefer to purchase a yearly worker's compensation plan. Since this insurance is typically tied to income and assuring the worker they will not lose this income when injured I am required to approach worker's compensation insurance in a different manner. At the start of each project I report the number of employees to the insurer rather than the amount of income paid. Then when they audit me at the end of the year I report that I paid out no income and the amount of money I owe for worker's compensation insurance is greatly reduced from what it would typically be.

g) It is not just Studio 804 that must be insured for a project to proceed. All the subcontractors must also be insured and have Property and Casualty Insurance that meets ACORD standards (Association of Cooperative Operations Research and Development). Since we often work with the same plumbers, electricians, mechanical contractors etc. these businesses have us on record and we have their ACORD documents that are updated by their provider to us every year. Through the standardized ACORD files, we are all assured that we are working with properly insured entities and not opening our business to undo risk. The yearly audit by the insurance company covering us reassures them we are not using anyone uninsured on our work site.

A
—
B C

A B C *The history of Studio 804 warehouses starts with my barn and ends in a fully equipped warehouse in the East Hills Business Park.*

D E

WAREHOUSE

I live on a farm outside Lawrence with the characteristic barns and outbuildings. I also have a workshop that I built with Rockhill and Associates and have expanded over the years to be well stocked for small scale fabrication. For the first nine years of Studio 804 when we needed storage or to do shop work this was our home. We stored equipment and materials in the unconditioned outbuilding and then cleared them of rodent nests when we needed them and brought them to the site. In the shop, we welded steel, did custom sheet metal fabrication and built mock-ups. We had to work around the crew of Rockhill and Associates who used the shop and outbuildings for the same purposes and we had to work around the farm being a farm. I have always had animals and the barn had horses and the chicken coop had chickens.

When we started working in Kansas City in 2004 on what became Mod 1 it was decided that we would prefabricate the house in Lawrence near the University and ship it to the site. This meant we needed a facility for building the modules and a location where they could conveniently be loaded for delivery. This was not a farm 15 miles outside Lawrence accessed by a dirt road. We could not afford to rent a fully outfitted warehouse, so we were

fortunate to find a vacant and derelict facility a few blocks from downtown Lawrence that we could use for very little money. It was rough and minimally conditioned, but at least we were indoors and had a secure place to put a job box packed with tools. We called this home for all four Mod houses. The challenges inherent to this warehouse directly shaped the design of the Mods. We had to get the prefabricated modules that made up the houses from the work space to the parking lot where they would be loaded by crane on to flatbed trailers. This path required passing through a garage door and navigating changes in direction and grade. This limited us in height, width, length and weight. It turned out to be a blessing in disguise as the limitations forced the students to think about design in ways they were not conditioned to in the all things are possible environment of most design studios.

Little did I know how good we had it in this warehouse until the owners decided they were ready to make improvements for their own use and we had to find a new location we could afford. We were working on the project for Greensburg, Kansas at the time and had to find something quickly. We ended up in an abandoned nitrogen fertilizer production plant warehouse on the outskirts of Lawrence that had recently closed. It was not an ideal work envi-

D E *The large amount of storage this facility can hold allowed me to say yes when Olson Kundig's office offered a collection of large glulam beams of varying sizes and lengths. I had no idea what we would do with them, but they were too nice to say no. We still have the beams and still think about using them regularly. They already served a temporary purpose when we used them to transform the warehouse into a symposium hall for an event that celebrated the first 20 years of Studio 804.*

ronment, it had no heat or toilets and we had to string up our own lights and set a panel and monitor our electric consumption. The only thing separating us from the winter weather was the 50-year-old sheet 29-gauge metal skin peppered with gaps and holes. If not for the fact that it mostly kept rain and snow off us and our work, it would have been more comfortable outside.

If the discomfort wasn't enough, since the plant was mostly vacant and dark at night and had become of favorite location for those who wanted to steal things they could turn into quick money, which unfortunately, included our tools and equipment on a few occasions.

By this time, Studio 804 was an internationally known program and Dean John Gaunt did not feel that this facility was sending the right message when an industry representative or the parents of a student would come to visit. In 2010 he decided to find Studio 804 a home befitting the program. He convinced the University of Kansas Endowment to purchase a large modern warehouse in a Lawrence business park that could be used by Studio 804 as well as all the other hands-on building efforts, big and small, that operate out of the architecture school.

At first, I was reticent, liking the image of the suffering artists working in horrid conditions to create art. But that was much more fun to talk about than experience and eventually I came to my senses. The day we moved into the East Hills Business Park warehouse was an important day in the evolution of Studio 804. We now have office space for the computer work and bookkeeping, we have a striking conference room where we meet with visitors and we have a large shop where any scale and any type of fabrication can occur. Another significant benefit is the vast amount of room for storage. The opportunity to purchase or salvage unique and useful materials might occur at any time even if we might not be able to immediately use them. In the past, we would have had to pass on these opportunities. The East Hills space allows us the freedom of long term storage of large amounts of material of about any size. We can then incorporate them into future designs when the opportunity and inspiration is right. For example, we purchased a large quantity of high performance insulated glass units for pennies on the dollar when a large high-profile project in Kansas City, Missouri was terminated after the glass units had already been fabricated. We stored them in the warehouse and have now used them on subsequent projects.

05

THE KANSAS CITY MODULAR HOUSES

As the operational model of Studio 804 became more predictable and stable the projects become more ambitious. I felt we had fully explored the possibilities with the Lawrence housing authorities and was looking for new ways to find and fund projects. Eventually this led to working in economically depressed areas of Kansas City, Kansas. Here we could get our work funded while still having the freedom to creatively design and build affordable housing in marginal neighborhoods.

Due to the logistics of working with University of Kansas students in Kansas City these houses were prefabricated in Lawrence and shipped to Kansas City in modules. The enthusiasm at the time for prefabrication architecture helped propel Studio 804 into the architectural spotlight as the projects received numerous awards and worldwide publication.

MOD 1, 2004

KANSAS CITY, KANSAS

THE KANSAS CITY MODULAR HOUSES

Kansas City, Kansas is the smaller cross border sibling to Kansas City, Missouri. The rise of the suburbs in the late twentieth century hit both urban areas hard but the Kansas side had farther to go to recover. The city was built on a rolling landscape that creates sweeping vistas and unique urban spaces. It has many grand old homes, elegantly designed parks and the kind of early twentieth century street adornment that creates a rich sense of place. But in the 2000s it was all covered in a depressing layer of decline. Widespread vacancy and decay hampered any attempt at revitalization. Even many of the people living in neighborhoods were surprised and doubtful when improvements were proposed.

Despite these concerns, I and others saw the potential in these derelict streets. We approached all nine of the CDC (Community Development Corporations) and explained our interest. We would be happy to provide the housing if they would provide temporary financial support despite the buildings looking a little different. We felt that the tide was turning for urban areas and that the population migration of the previous forty years was about to reverse. Mod 1 was an effort to prove it. It was a cooperative venture that brought together Studio 804, the urban developers City Vision Ministries (CVM), the Rosedale Development Association (RDA) and Unified Government of Wyandotte County and Kansas City Kansas to develop a project on a vacant lot in the Rosedale neighborhood. It is only a couple of minutes from the University of Kansas Medical Center and the thriving entertainment and restaurant district at 39th and State Line. This was just one of many pockets of recent urban revitalization on both sides of the state line. I was confident that there would be young people looking for a first house who would feel the positives outweighed the perceived negatives of buying a house in this location.

CVM helped us find a site and then with the RDA cleaned it up to create a viable, safe place for a house. Since we were building the house in Lawrence the CVM paid for the foundation and built it to our specifications. Beyond this they left the design and execution of the house to us. All the parties involved agreed that dwellings built to underlying modernist principles could be interspersed in these old neighborhoods. Rather than being perceived as interlopers the buildings would be received as optimistic beacons of change with the potential to stimulate further development. Everyone's faith was proven wise when the house sold before we were finished and it played its part in the further development of the Rosedale neighborhood which has gone through dramatic, positive change in the 20 years since.

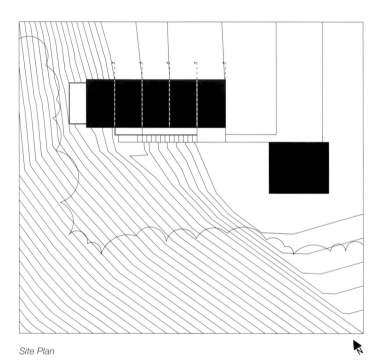

Site Plan

B *When I first met with the City Vision Ministries, Kansas City, Kansas and Wyandotte County was facing an uphill battle when it came to the effort to revitalize their struggling urban neighborhoods. The blight that existed in the early 21st century had been a 70-year process that had gained momentum in the 1960s through the 90s as the exodus to the suburbs hit its peak. Many neighborhoods were burdened with dozens of derelict, abandoned houses or vacant un-maintained lots and even more that had fallen from the tax rolls. It created a general sense of decay and made it hard to get developers to invest in something new.*

C D *The property had been an impromptu landfill at the dead end of a residential street. It is at the edge of a ridge that drops quickly to the interstate and industrial bottom land. The house is screened from the noise below by a healthy stand of trees.*

A
—
B C D

E F G *For two months, we built the modular units in the Van Go, Inc. warehouse and then used industrial casters that we improvised to roll them out the garage door.*

PREFABRICATION

Once we had the site and funding I had to decide how to go about building a house in Kansas City. If a project is going to be mass produced or is being built on a site isolated from supplies and a stable work force prefabrication makes sense logistically and financially. For a custom one-time project, it is usually more efficient to build on site and avoid all the complications of moving the units and designing it to withstand the move. This was not a typical situation. The students were based 40 miles away from the Rosedale Neighborhood and were connected by a busy interstate that became a congested mess during each morning and evening rush hour. I did not like the thought of tired students driving back and forth each day on dark winter roads. It was not safe, and over a semester it would accumulate into a gross waste of time that could be better spent otherwise.

To prefabricate the buildings in Lawrence meant that we had to devise a process. Was it one large mobile home like unit or built in parts? How would the mechanical, electrical and plumbing systems be integrated? We had to research the restriction in moving the units on the highways and side roads, figure out how to set it in place, and probably most important-ly, we had to have a place to do the prefabrication. It had to be somewhere easily accessible for the crane and trucks that were going to be used to move the house and I felt it would be nice to work indoors for a change. Due to the school schedule,

most of Studio 804's on site work happens in the heart of the Kansas winter and this is quite a shock for a student who has never experienced trying to do difficult work while cold and wearing gloves and layers of clothing.

WORKING IN A WAREHOUSE

We were able to rent a 10,000 square-foot warehouse in Lawrence owned by Van Go Inc. - a local art's program that works to support disadvantaged youth. It became our home to prefabricate the units. The highway restrictions limited our design options, but no more than the warehouse did. We not only had to be able to transport the building, but we had to get it out of the warehouse garage doors.

We quickly learned about some of the complication of prefab-ricating a building in one city and placing it in another. The Uni-fied Government of Kansas City, Kansas and Wyandotte County was not going to send an inspector to Lawrence to inspect the mechanical, plumbing, electrical and structural compliance before it was covered up with drywall. We had to hire a third party to inspect the work as it proceeded in the warehouse. Prefabrication taught the students about codes in a unique way. They can easily look up the information about most typical construction techniques, but when you prefabricate a building some issues such as anchoring the building to the foundation become much more difficult. It is harder, if not impossible to find black and white answers for these code questions.

THE FIVE BAY DESIGN

The five modules were all the same size and each housed a functional component of the house. First, was the living module, then the kitchen module, then a bathroom utility module followed by two modules that are bedrooms. The result is a streamlined 1,200 square-foot, two-bedrooms, one-bathroom house with a large cantilevered deck and a full basement with the potential for later development. The kitchen uses affordable but contemporary Ikea cabinetry and the appliances are all stainless steel. The bathroom walls are clad with salvaged aluminium and the floors throughout are rapidly renewable vertical grain bamboo.

When Studio 804 started building houses I struggled with the students preconceived notions of what a house should be and their training in design studios that tended to promote grandiose individualistic thinking. A restrained, minimal aesthetic was not part of their design language. It had not occurred to me until we started Mod 1 that the design limitations of prefabrication would ironically be liberating. The fact that our modules had to be able to fit around street corners, under bridges and power lines and through the warehouse doors meant there were few options when it came to the building form. Also, for the same reasons we were prefabricating in the first place, we had to keep on site work to a minimum since we would be driving there each day. This meant we were not going to add unnecessary architectural components. These conditions helped me convince the students to focus their design efforts on the tectonics of the building. It was an important breakthrough in development of Studio 804, which was reinforced when the house won international design awards and was published world-wide.

We continued to use rainscreens because they not only make functionally better buildings but also give us wide ranging freedom to try unique sidings. In this case, we used 1 x 2 strips of massaranduba. It is a Brazilian hardwood and was certified by the Sierra Club and the Forest Stewardship Council (FSC) as an environmentally approved material. We mitered the corners and secured the horizontally run strips with stainless steel screws. The wood has a warm red/brown colour at the time of installation. It will naturally turn gray over time but we decided to treat it with a penetrating clear finish in hopes of keeping the fresh cut colour for as long as possible.

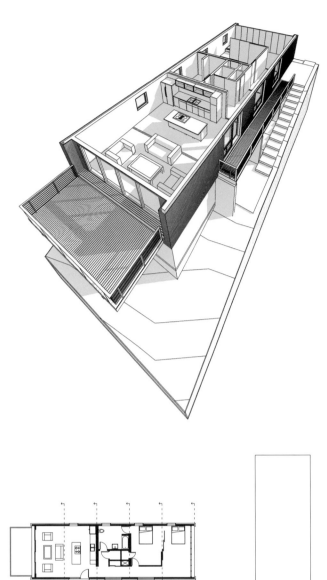

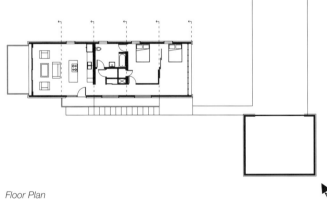

Floor Plan

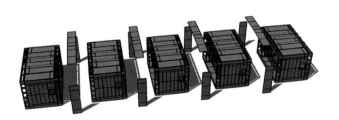

H *We built five wood framed modules complete with wall finishes, cabinetry, windows and siding. Once they were secured to the foundation they simply had to be stitched together. This was made much easier by the layered rainscreen cladding.*

I J K *The modules were moved to the warehouse parking lot where each bay was loaded onto its own flatbed truck and transported to the site in Kansas City. Upon arrival, they were placed on the foundation that had been finished to our specifications by a concrete sub-contractor, one of the few times we let someone else do our concrete work.*

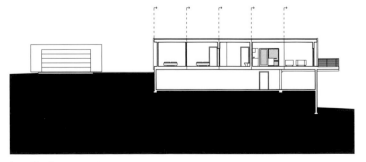

Long Section

I
H J K

MOD 2, 2005

Rosedale Neighborhood, Kansas City, Kansas

PLANTING ANOTHER SEED

Following the successful completion of Mod 1, Mod 2 sought to expand upon the lessons learned. Issues of transportation, tectonics, accessibility, siting, and building delivery continued to drive the process. As with Mod 1 it was a cooperative venture with City Vision Ministries (CVM) and the Rosedale Development Association (RDA) We continued to work to help ease the urgent community need for entry-level housing and we again did it in a neglected neighborhood hoping to plant another seed in the eventual re-growth of the urban fabric weakened by vacant lots and buildings and all the problems that follow.

The class of 2005 started by trying to find a piece of property that would allow them to fulfil the mission for the program that had been cemented by their predecessors. The Unified Government of Kansas City, Kansas and Wyandotte County, like many communities, has a program to acquire properties that might otherwise go vacant. Most often this is triggered when the owners are delinquent on their tax payments. The city then encourages development by selling the properties to qualified and willing builders at minimal cost. The Land Bank, as it is known in this case, sold us the property for $300. Once we had established ourselves as a program and were a proven presence in their community they donated the properties. This was the most significant reason we decided to continue working in Kansas City rather than Lawrence - despite the hassles of the commute.

A *Each dot represents 5 vacant lots (vacant of structure or tax payment) in Kansas City, Kansas and Wyandotte County in 2004. It fit Studio 804s mission to help this community reverse this crippling situation.*

B
——
A

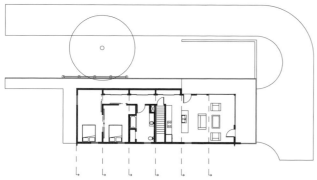

Floor Plan

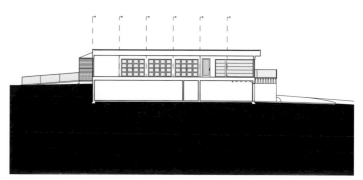

Section

DESIGN

Mod 2 is made up of six prefabricated modules that create a 1,200 square-foot two-bedroom, one-bath single-family house. We again built the units in the same Lawrence warehouse we used for Mod 1 and transported them by truck to the site where they were placed on a concrete foundation that had been prepared to our specifications. As with Mod 1, building the foundations, the full basement walls and necessary retaining walls for the sloped site would have been too time consuming for the students to complete in our one semester window. We needed all hands working on the prefabrication of the units. This did not set well with me as I wanted the students involved in all parts of the process.

CVM insisted that the house have an enclosed garage. Mod 1 and its detached garage had worked well but this time I was determined to hide the garage door. The street facing gaping mouth of a garage is symbolic of so many facets of American culture that need to be changed - such as the over emphasis on the car, the sedentary lifestyle and the fading of neighborhood connections. It did not fit the avowed mission of Studio 804 to play a part in this so we took advantage of the sloping site to hide the garage door. The house sits on top of a walk out basement. The top of the basement is nearly at grade level at the front of the house but by the back it is fully exposed. A driveway ramps down from the street behind a retaining wall that creates a level side yard. It then U-turns toward the back of the house where a garage door has been installed in the exposed basement wall hiding under the deck above. This solution also saved precious on-site time since the garage was part of the foundation that was ready for us when we arrived.

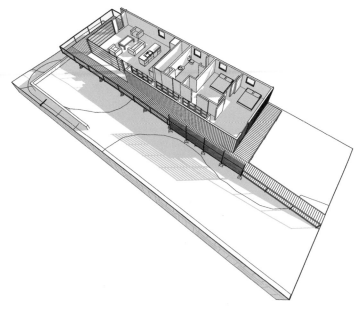

C E G
F
D

To enter the house from the street an ipe floored elevated walkway parallels the house to the entry. It then wraps around the back of the house to a deck that looks over the surprisingly isolated back yard and woods behind. The deck railings are custom welded with as innocuous a steel frame as possible that holds clear, tempered glass panels. We wanted the living room to open to this deck, so the public living areas are at the back of the house while the bedrooms and support spaces are toward the front. The living room, kitchen and entry are housed in three modules of open space except for an enclosed opening in the floor behind the kitchen that allowed us to site build a staircase down to the garage and basement. A hallway extends from the entry to the private spaces. It is flanked on one side by a module wide bathroom and a module wide bedroom, on the other side are built in storage cabinets with custom built doors. At the end of the hallway is a full module size master bedroom at the front of the house.

Our default design setting is to open our houses to the south for passive solar heat gain but in this instance the lay of the site and the prominent views to the woods made this less attractive. We chose to focus on other sustainable strategies such as cross ventilation, daylighting and the use of salvaged materials and then find a way to turn a northeast facing living room into a positive. We did this by taking advantage of the soft north light to daylight the living room and kitchen through a fully glazed corner fabricated with 250 square feet of horizontally run structural channel glass. A translucent, thermally broken structural glazing designed by Bendheim Glass for Steven Holl's Bloch addition to the Nelson-Atkins Museum of Art in Kansas City, Missouri. The glass from the mock ups and fritting experiments was being held in the storage yard of Carter Glass who was installing the channels at the Nelson for Bendheim. Carter Glass had already developed a relationship with Studio 804 and helped us secure the donation of the channel glass and then helped the students with installation details. This would be one of many examples I use to explain to students the value of the knowledge people in the field can bring to a project. All too often architects fail to see the contribution the trades can bring to a project's success. It is an important lesson of the 804 experience; to respect and learn from people who work in the building industry daily.

D *Storage is always a challenge when designing or living in a small house. In this case I challenged the students to turn storage into a design asset. We milled maple stiles and rails and used polycarbonate infill panels to create a run of doors that are one of unique features of the house.*

E F G *The structural glass channel we used was left over from the experiments with different fritting treatments as Bendheim and Steven Holl's office worked to perfect the "lanterns" that were central to the design of the Bloch Building, an addition to the Nelson-Atkins Museum of Art in Kansas City, Missouri.*

MATERIALS

Since prefabrication was leading to designs of a minimalist aesthetic it brought added focus to the material choices and their detailing. It forced the students to confront these tectonic issues in a more serious way than they were used to. In addition to the successful use of the structural glass channel other materials that define the building as more than a mundane box are the salvaged maple, tongue and groove wood gymnasium flooring, the aluminum storefront window systems and salvaged aluminum trim, the clean lined Ikea cabinetry and the PaperStone countertops made using water-based resins to shape a recycled paper mass. PaperStone was still a relatively new company at the time and we were excited to be able to work with them on an affordable house. Working with these suppliers and manufactures on donations or favorable pricing not only saves us money but also brings awareness to these new materials and helps make them more accessible and eventually more affordable.

H *The house is clad with a cypress wood rainscreen detailed with recycled aluminum trim and flashings*

I *We used nearly every square inch of potential volume while still getting the module out of the garage door at the warehouse.*

SELLING MOD 2

No matter how well a house is designed the project is not really a success until it is sold. The CVM and RDA are experienced at packaging houses in these urban neighborhoods for sale. Not only do they have a network to get the word out about the house's availability, but they also have the connections to assist first-time home buyers qualify for financing and government assistance. They work with programs like Neighborworks America who works to create public and private partnerships at local levels to support affordable housing. Mod 2 was sold sight unseen since we were still working in the warehouse prefabricating the models. We had sold two projects in Kansas City with nearly no effort and without a realtor. I realized we had stumbled upon a very good way to operate.

K *The house is clad with a cypress wood rainscreen detailed with recycled aluminum trim and flashings.*

MOD 3, 2006

Strawberry Hill Neighborhood, Kansas City, Kansas

EL CENTRO

Mod 3 was constructed in the historic Strawberry Hill Neighborhood of Kansas City, Kansas. It sits on top of a pronounced
hill and has an expansive view of the Kansas City, Missouri
skyline. The site inspired us to try and create a building equal
to its potential. I often see mediocre or worse buildings on sen-
sational sites and wonder how anyone who calls themselves
an architect allows it to happen. I did not want others looking
at this house and thinking the same thing.

City Vision Ministries was not able to fund another house when
the class of 2006 convened. El Centro, Inc. stepped in to fill
the void. They are a not-for-profit whose mission is strengthening communities and improving lives of Latinos and others
through educational, social, and economic opportunities.
They were interested in supporting efforts to build affordable
housing in their community and were familiar with our work.
The first two Mods had sold with ease and El Centro felt as I
did that we could continue this recipe and create exceptional
housing that was both good for Studio 804 and the neighborhoods. Since we were starting this new funding relationship
it seemed like an opportune time to secure more from the
process for Studio 804. It seemed possible, if I played things
right that Studio 804 would eventually be able to develop our
own speculative projects. This would significantly lessen the
year to year anxiety to get started. El Centro understood and
was cooperative. They agreed to loan us the money for construction for six months with a guaranteed pay back of eight
percent when the property sold. If the market value supported
a higher selling price the rest of money would help fund future
Studio 804 projects.

KEEPING A LOW PROFILE

I had learned from years of working on houses with Rockhill and Associates, as well as the first few with Studio 804, that if you are going to design houses that do not conform to many people's conservative expectations of what a house should be you need to carefully manage the way neighborhoods first learn of your project. You want to introduce the work on your terms. Seemingly, every neighborhood has its self-proclaimed watch dogs and if they catch wind of a development before it has been shared they see it as their responsibility to inform everyone and most likely not in the terms you would choose. This usually arouses those who are suspicious of development or simply against change. With the ability to use social media and its specious relationship to the facts they can rally like-minded troops and any project that needs public support at any phase can get away from you before you have even had a chance to form a proposal.

I am not suggesting developers and architects should surprise attack neighborhoods and circumvent the concerns of the neighbors. These neighborhood organizations and those who lead them do valuable work and give voice to those who might otherwise be ignored, especially amongst populations that are not the focus of most political campaigns. Instead, I have found that when we get to shape the first impression by setting up a neighborhood meeting and allowing the students to present our design and reasons behind it we are typically greeted with respect and good will. There will always be those against change and those who want all work to satisfy their tastes but when we build off a foundation of support amongst a core group of neighbors it becomes much easier to refute concerns when we are seeking local approvals. It also makes for a more pleasant job site when those you are working amongst are on your side.

Our neighbors may have thought we were nuts for building in the neighborhood, but this was okay with us. At least they were not against our being there or felt it was their role to determine how our house would look.

This lesson did not take hold early enough for the students building Mod 3. They were looking at several properties available in the land bank and were particularly excited about the potential of one location. It was in a neighborhood that would require historic guidelines be respected and the associated public reviews negotiated. In their enthusiasm, they descended on the site in large numbers to take measurements, shoot pictures and document the surroundings. Since for years, little new construction had occurred in the area this provoked interest and it did not take much detective work to figure out who the students were and what they were doing. Soon, residents were going door to door sharing their concerns about how our work might impact the neighborhood. Our mission to create sustainable, affordable housing fell to the wayside. The concerns focused primarily on the appearance of the houses and how they were different from the surroundings - even though the neighborhood gained much of its distinction through its rich collection of early to mid-twentieth century architecture of many styles.

Once this had occurred the angry voices had control of the narrative and it was quickly and publicly decided that we were not welcome. As a last hope, El Centro set up a neighborhood meeting to try to reverse the incoming tide of resistance but by the second speaker I knew we were doomed. I do not understand the psychology behind it, but several times during my

career, including this day, I have heard the argument that modern design attracts undesirables, or during one memorable town hall meeting, perverts. No matter how good it might have felt to prevail, Studio 804 did not have the time to fight this battle. The design was going to have to be approved by the local historic review board and as entrenched as many of the neighbors were against our work I felt it was too risky to continue with the potential for delays and redesign time.

STRAWBERRY HILL
So now it was March and we were back to square one and looking for a piece of property. I was a bit panicked at the time, but it turned out to be a fortunate turn of events. Through the land bank we found the much less contentious site on Strawberry Hill. We chose to work here even though the surroundings were derelict – even for the type of sites we had been working on. There were several boarded-up houses close by, including one next door. When I first visited, a patriarch of the neighborhood greeted me. He was incredulous when I told him what we were doing. He waved his hand toward the neighborhood telling me there were dozens of houses that had been for sale for years for less money than we would be asking. I didn't have the heart to tell him I was quite certain that we would sell the house before it was built.

THE CONCRETE PIERS
Mod 3 is perched on top of a hill well above the street like a bird surveying the surroundings - but ready to take flight at any moment. It was the effect we had in mind when we decided to place it on eight concrete piers. This not only allowed the building to tread lightly on the site, but it allowed us to do the foundation work ourselves within our tight window of time. The only work we had to sub contract was the excavation as I did not have a large enough auger to create the bearing surface for the footings that engineering had deemed necessary. Once that was done the students set the formwork and poured the footings and concrete piers. I take pride in the all-inclusive nature of the Studio 804 experience and hated having to subcontract something as essential as the foundations the previous two years.

We poured the concrete piers and then spanned them with two parallel steel beams that cantilever beyond each end and reinforce the floating appearance of the house when viewed from below. The six prefabricated modules were placed on the beams and ganged. For Mod 3 we pressed the "less is more" aesthetic even further than before. We felt a clean, simple box perched in the sky would be more powerful than a house with additive elements like decks or overhangs cluttering the composition.

The local building department was not receptive to our choice to use the concrete piers. When we submitted for a building permit the design was rejected. If we were going to continue with this submittal we were required to have the design approved and stamped by a structural engineer. At least Studio 804 had a developing relationship with a structural engineer who understood the program and embraced the occasional craziness of our ideas and schedule. He quickly turned around a stamped set so we could re-submit and move forward. Unfortunately, there was little intention of letting us easily proceed. Our engineer was then required to submit all his calculations, and despite the obvious insult he complied.

Though these experiences are difficult I remind myself that this is an important part of what Studio 804 offers the students. They are required to take thoughtful stands based on documented evidence rather than just arguing opinions. The forces of conformity come from many directions and there are many times it will be easier to relent and do what is requested – especially if one is not confident in their work. To easily concede is often not best for the individuals or communities being served. This was emphatically the case with Mod 3. Once it was completed the house won numerous design awards including Architect Magazine's Home of Year and probably is our most published project worldwide. More importantly its presence started a bit of a renaissance as neighbors became inspired to work on their properties, even if was just cleaning up the yard, and over the next couple of years' copycat "modern" developments by local builders started happening on nearby vacant properties as others hoped to profit on the same formula we had found.

THE LAYOUT

The six modules create an efficient 1,200 square-foot, two-bedroom house. The first two modules that face the street hold the living room and deck. The next two modules support the wet spaces with a galley kitchen facing one exterior wall and the bathroom, laundry and a mechanical space facing the other. The two modules at the back create the bedrooms, one made flexible with a moving storage wall. The windows were located throughout to promote cross ventilation and control solar penetration. To make the small floor plan feel more generous we used surface mounted sliding doors rather than swing doors which would consume a large part of the room to clear for their swing. The exterior is clad with a rainscreen using a Vaproshield barrier and douglas fir wood strips.

The minimal approach extended to the site. It was expressive enough without our help. We built a concrete retaining wall along the sidewalk broken by an opening at the bottom for a concrete staircase composed of 24 poured in place steps. At the top of the hill a sidewalk connects the house, garage and driveway. Opposite the house on the other side of the sidewalk is a large existing walnut tree that balances the composition from the street.

```
____C D
A B
```

A B C D *The modules were framed using a prefabricated wood truss floor frame. This kept the weight down and allowed us to run the mechanical system through the floor while still having enough depth to properly insulate the belly of the elevated house. The wood cribbing between the concrete piers are carrying the load of the units until the concrete that was poured the day before had time to gain strength.*

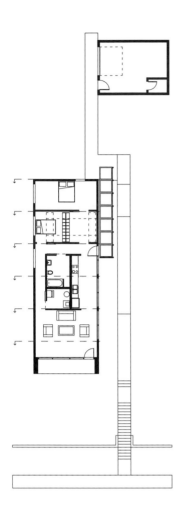

Floor Plan

N

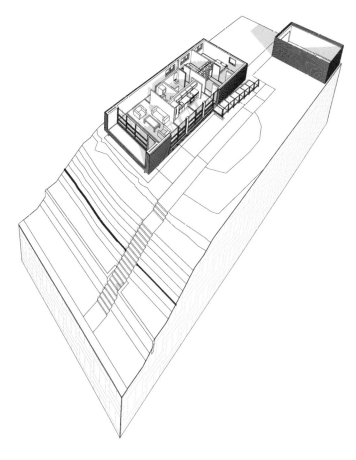

E H
F G

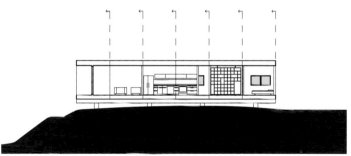

E F G *We felt it was important to have a deck looking toward the skyline view but did not want an additive deck cluttering the simple form we desired. To achieve both goals we ended up incorporating the deck into a module rather than adding it on site as we had done before. This became one of the identifiable characteristics of the house and minimized on site construction time.*

MOD 4, 2007

Rosedale Neighborhood, Kansas City, Kansas

GETTING STARTED

We were having a hard time finding a land bank property that fit the goals I had set for the 2007 class. The constant angst and uncertainty surrounding the funding of each year's project was wearing on me and I had to find an alternative. I was seriously pursing the financial independence that would allow us to develop our own projects, but we were not there yet. In the meantime, we had pursued every imaginable avenue to fund projects including many foundations who seemed willing to support us. The problem was our very tight time frame. It does not fit comfortably with the way many of these groups operate. Needing the money yesterday and being done tomorrow was not their way. Fortunately, El Centro was happy to fund the construction of another house for a small percentage return while allowing Studio 804 to sell the house at market value. This added to our incentive to sell the property for as much as possible while still living up to our social mission.

The Rosedale neighborhood alerted us to a potential seller for a piece of property near the University of Kansas Medical Center. This was exactly where I hoped to work. We would still be building in a recovering neighborhood, but we would be within walking distance of several employers, restaurants and neighborhood facilities. Amazingly, considering it was in the middle of an established urban neighborhood, the property was nearly three acres at the end of a dead-end road with a significant wooded area that supported wildlife. Not surprisingly there was a reason it was available. Long ago it had been a community landfill. We would be building on the soil that covered the refuse. This would of course create challenges with the foundation, but it also gave us an opportunity to responsibly develop a brownfield site and make it affordable.

The class of 2007 met for the first time in August of 2006 and was the first class I had for an entire school year. Studio 804 was proving to be a success and the work was bringing attention to the architecture program at the University of Kansas. I felt we were only scratching the surface of what the program could do. One of the limitations was the amount of work that could be done in one semester, especially when Studio 804 was only one of several responsibilities. The revised track for a master's degree in architecture required the students to fulfil all their obligations other than studio before they started their final year. This was done to support my program as well as other budding building and intern programs at the school. Now I had the students for nine months with few school obligations.

With the added time I wanted the class of 2007 to explore a larger prefabricated house than the previous Mods and I wanted to do more than simply re-package the typical three-bedroom house. I challenged the students to design a house that

could accommodate a family while still being flexible enough to appeal to the urban couples who had been drawn to our work in Kansas City thus far. I wanted the house to be able to adapt to the terms of the buyer, not the other way around. When Mod 4 was finished, I wanted the visiting appraiser or family to tour a three-bedroom house. When the young childless urbanites arrived, I wanted them to tour a one-bedroom house with loft living qualities.

The added square-footage and the potential for more bedrooms would not only add to the market for the house by appealing to a wider demographic but also by making a bank mortgage easier to attain. Even though we were reaching a more sophisticated audience it was still true that infill projects in these neighborhoods were not likely to attract buyers with the resources at hand to buy the house outright. They were going to have to secure financial assistance and loans. Banking and the appraisal system had changed little since we started in Lawrence. They still worked from the same formulas and the only comparables were our own work of the last three years and we were planning to exceed those in value.

DESIGN

This was the project where sustainability became more to us than using common sense passive strategies with salvaged and recycled materials. LEED was emerging and Rockhill and Associates became accredited that year. LEED for Homes was still years away, but it made me more aware of comprehensive ways to think about sustainability and I wanted to pursue several of these practices. Building on this site was exactly the type of work LEED was promoting. It was an infill site and it was a brownfield that needed to be brought back into use. We could split the site in to two properties and still have the required street frontage to meet city zoning requirements. To be able to get a building permit on these sites we had to have geo-technical engineering done to determine the depth of the foundations and the bearing surface required. Mod 4 was built on the first site reached at the end of Lloyd Street which was at the highest point of the site and required the least amount of foundation work. We have yet to develop the second property but if we ever do it will require piers over 20' deep to reach a stable bearing surface.

Since I was selling this house hoping to fund future work we had to offset the added costs of buying the property as well as the complications related to the foundation. This put even more pressure on the design to deepen the potential buying market. The result was a 1,500 square-foot flexible three-bedroom, two-bath house composed of seven modules. At seven modules, the house was starting to get very long if the bays were just lined up like books on a shelf. We also felt this house should have a stronger connection to its large site than the previous Mods which were more view oriented and were objects on the landscape. A long shoe box would not create outdoor spaces. To address this concern, we offset the module by four-foot between the three module public spaces and four module private rooms. This shift created outdoor spaces catty corner to each other with the entry ramp at one corner near the street and a south facing deck at the other corner adjacent to the living room. With this

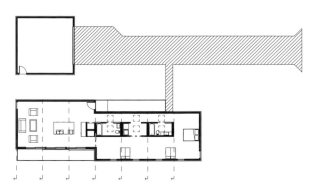

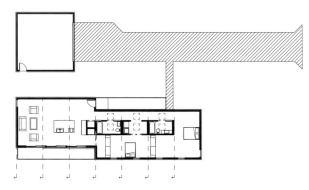

Floor Plan – One Bedroom Layout

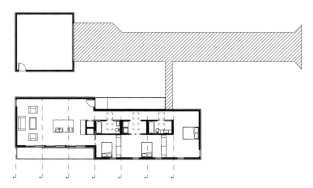

Floor Plan – Two-bedroom Layout

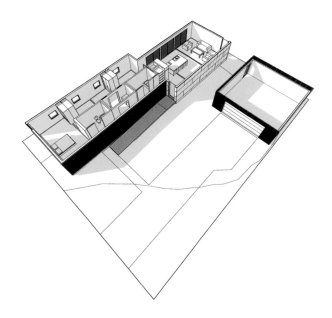

Floor Plan – Three-bedroom Layout

simple shift in the plan these exterior spaces now seem to fill the void in the form rather than being applied. The shift in plan was further enhanced by having the four private modules cantilever off the foundation on the side opposite the entry.

The entry ramp leads to the three modules that hold the living room and an open kitchen, they exit to the deck through large sliding doors on the south elevation. The private modules can be accessed on either side of a wet core that hold the support spaces. One hall leads to the bathrooms and laundry. On the south side of the core is the flex space that can be organized with movable storage units to create one or two-bedrooms or as a single office space open to the living area as well as the master bedroom that fills the final module.

SUSTAINABLE DESIGN

Even though it was not until the next year's class that we submitted for LEED certification this was the first project where we began to inventory our materials and design choices with an eye toward entering the house in the growing number of competitions such as the Green Good Design Awards which focus on sustainable architecture. Mod 4 used some of the materials we had used before such as rapidly renewable bamboo for flooring, countertops made with recycled content, cellulose insulation and highly reflective white membrane roofing. We also once again exploited the long southern exposure for passive solar heating and situated the opening to promote cross ventilation. But, with this house we expanded on these efforts in a more comprehensive way. Half of the house was clad with a rainscreen made of Forest Stewardship Council (FSC) certified lumber. The other half was clad with recycled aluminum panels. The play between these two created a rich contrast between the forms and gave a bold presence to the relatively simple composition.

H I
___
J

Rather than rely on fixed louver which can be undermined by unseasonable weather we allowed the home owner to control the amount of the sun's heat and light that enters the house. They can move large panels that pass in front of the glass sliding doors and track with barn door hardware. The panels match the cumaru rainscreen and when they are closed filtered daylight passes between the tightly spaced horizontal boards. The house can be opened to the prevailing breezes with large south windows and cross ventilated through the typical smaller windows high on the north walls and operable skylights. Another striking sustainable feature is pervious paving for the sidewalks and driveway. It was the first time we used one of these products, in this case a plastic gridded product that transfers the traffic loads to gravel below and assures that the dirt in each cell does not become compacted and unable to support the growth of a ground cover. Not only does this pavement eliminate storm water runoff and reduce the use of concrete but it also obscures the driveway, turning it into a part of the lawn and reducing the visual impact of the car on the site.

J *The decks are supported by steel frames that rest on cantilevered steel beams. This kept the exterior vocabulary as minimal as possible and avoided further foundation work. The deck heights are low enough to forego the use of railings.*

06

THE PIVOTAL YEAR

The class of 2008 was a pivotal one in the development of Studio 804. Not only did they do the first commercial building after years of residences, but it was the first in what is now 10 LEED Platinum certified buildings. Through the work of Studio 804 and Rockhill and Associates I have become increasingly dedicated to exploring sustainable design. I have tried to incorporate passive strategies for heating and cooling since the beginning of my practice and have always used salvaged material, mostly for very practical cost concerns.

Early efforts to add active systems such as wind turbines, photovoltaics and geo-thermal heating and cooling were sidetracked. Usually by the upfront costs associated with them. There would be support during the design process but when it came time to finalize the budget these components were viewed as add-ons. They were easy targets for cost reduction. In Greensburg, with its post tornado mission to aggressively build green, this was less likely to be the case.

547 ARTS CENTER, 2008

Greensburg, Kansas
LEED Platinum Certified

MAY 4, 2007

Kansas is known for tornadoes. They most often start when warm moist air from the Gulf of Mexico meets dry air moving east from the desert southwest. The warm moist air rises above the dryer air and this layering creates the conditions that a storm needs. On 4 May 2007, there was a particularly large variance between the air masses that met over the Central States. That afternoon the National Oceanic and Atmospheric Administration (NOAA) Storm Prediction Center issued a risk notice for severe storms. By that evening the supercells that led to an outbreak of over 100 tornadoes across Kansas over a three-day period had started to form. One of these tornadoes struck Greensburg at 9.45pm that first night and destroyed 95 percent of the town.

A B

B *For a tornado to hit Greensburg was an astounding stroke of bad luck. From Pratt, Kansas to Dodge City is 76 miles connected by US Route 54. This stretch of highway is sparsely populated and is mostly open land with the occasional grain silo visible on the far horizon signaling a small community of a few hundred at most.*

That night the people of Greensburg were under a tornado warning for 39 minutes and NOAA issued a tornado emergency message telling the residents to take cover ten minutes before the storm hit. It was later classified an EF5 tornado, the maximum damage potential rating on the Enhanced Fujita Scale. It was 1.7 miles wide (wider than Greensburg itself) and had surface winds of at least 205 miles per hour. It was on the ground for 65 minutes and travelled 28.8 miles. During the last few of these miles it went directly down the main street of Greensburg ripping the warning siren from its perch and leaving almost total destruction. Despite the reputation of being in the middle of tornado alley Kansas has only had to absorb six such storms since 1950 and in May of 2007 there had not been an EF5 tornado in the United States since the 1999 storm that devastated Moore, Oklahoma.[1]

In 2007, Greensburg had a population of approximately 1400 people. It was the Kiowa County seat and the location of the courthouse, library and county hospital. Along with the county functions its economy depended on the agriculture, oil and gas industries. It was a typical early 21st century Kansas town. Like most rural Kansas towns, Greensburg was in decline when the tornado hit. It had been losing population for decades and it was easy to wonder if the town should be rebuilt at all – or if so, to what capacity. The county seat could be moved elsewhere and Greensburg could be left as a stop on the highway.

Those that wanted to stay and rebuild knew it was going to require vision and a plan. They had to come up with a way to generate economic growth as well as create a sense of excitement and pride in Greensburg that would keep the young from moving away - already a challenge before the tornado. In meetings in tents set up on the courthouse lawn city leaders decided that if you were going to start over you might as well try to make the city better than it was before. In a part of country where little attention had been paid to light pollution or xeriscaping they had the foresight to see that they could distinguish themselves from other rural towns, gain international attention, save the community operating money and, if all

went well, spark economic growth not often seen on the great plains by embracing "green design". Sustainable design was gaining mainstream momentum in America and it had become a subject that sparked passion in the young people Greensburg hoped to keep or attract. "Putting the green in Greensburg" was a cooperative effort between the citizens of Greensburg, Kiowa county, the Kansas governor's office and the Kansas division of Emergency Management as well as federal representatives from Federal Emergency Management Agency (FEMA), the United States Department of Agriculture (USDA) Rural Development office, the Environmental Protection Agency (EPA) and Department of Energy (DOE).

Initially there was resistance to the added upfront costs and all the certification paper work associated with LEED. Despite this the town leaders pushed forward and, in the end, mandated that all city owned buildings of more than 4,000 square feet be built to the highest of LEED standards[2]. It was an unprecedented effort and has in most every way proven to be successful.

The city boasts more LEED Platinum buildings per capita than any city in the world[3] and has recovered much of its tax base. It operates off 100 percent renewable electricity and in 2010-11 The DOE and the National Renewable Energy Laboratory (NREL) did post occupancy testing on 13 Greensburg buildings and determined that the city was saving a total of $200,000 in energy costs per year. One of these buildings was the 547 Arts Center built by Studio 804[4].

THE CLASS OF 2008
The open house for Studio 804s 2007 project Mod 4 occurred shortly after the tornado had hit Greensburg. It was on people's minds as they visited and several suggested that Studio 804 consider doing work in Greensburg. At that time, it was dismissed as well intentioned but not realistic. It seemed to be too soon after the tornado to be approaching Greensburg about developing a project. I was also wary of taking students on the road, let alone working in a disaster area. It was full of red flags.

In August of 2007 the 2008 class began the process of developing or finding the next project. They were severely hampered as the greatest world financial crises since the great depression was gaining momentum and by the time the class gathered the housing market was in free fall. By November of 2007 it was becoming obvious that a project in Kansas City or Lawrence like we had been doing was not likely. Eventually the discussion of working in Greensburg was revived. Two students went to visit and see what potential there was for a project that could start almost immediately. They were well received and everyone decided it would be beneficial to make a presentation to the city and Studio 804 was added to the agenda for December 2007.

Rural Kansas is typically Kansas State University territory, both in sports fandom and in what is viewed as the cultural divide between the universities. Kansas State is rural with an agricultural history and Lawrence is thought of as more Eastern, a part of the cultural elite. The truth is they are quite similar but the stereotypes persist. It probably fit this narrative when Studio 804 showed city leader's examples of the previous class's work which had little in common with the typical building done in rural Kansas. Despite the doubts and any lingering rivalries, the people of Greensburg did not want to turn away the offer of immediate work that would be done for a reasonable price.

1) National Oceanic and Atmospheric Administration (NOAA), PDF "Facts about the May 4, 2007 Greensburg Tornado and F5 and EF5 Tornadoes of the United States 1950-present" available at the NOAA website: www.noaa.gov .

2) United States Department of Energy, "Rebuilding it Better: Greensburg, Kansas High Performance Buildings Meeting Energy Savings Goals." April 2012, p 2.

3) Quinn, Patrick, "After devastating tornado, town is reborn 'green'," USA Today Green Living Magazine (www.usatoday.com), April 13, 2013.

4) United States Department of Energy, "Rebuilding it Better: Greensburg, Kansas High Performance Buildings Meeting Energy Savings Goals." p 1.

5) NOAA, "Facts about the May 4, 2007 Greensburg Tornado and F5 and EF5 Tornadoes of the United States 1950-present."

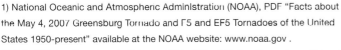

C D *Google Earth images of Greensburg, Kansas before and after.*

E *Due to the early warning and the fact that Kansan's know tornadoes only 11 people were killed, but 961 houses or business were destroyed. Nearly every tree was uprooted or twisted so severely it would not survive. 800,000 cubic yards of debris had to be removed before repairs could begin. Storms of this size are not common[5].*

F *Studio 804 was chosen to build the city's arts center. This was unexpected as the list of projects needed was long – including nearly every type of building that composes a town. The FEMA tents were still up and housing most community functions. The hospital looked like an army tent out of the movie M.A.S.H.*

G *The building has continued to serve our short and long-term goals. It is a living room for the community. They not only use if for city commission meetings but also as a place to gather for events and it acts as a gallery presenting regional works of art.*

H
—
I J

I As the project got closer to completion the visits from various network news shows and regional dignitaries become a regular event. This included a drive by visit from the President George W. Bush and a more enthusiastically received on-site visit from members of the University of Kansas men's basketball team which had just won the national championship.

J The Discovery Channel filmed a documentary about the rebuilding of Greensburg. Being as our project would be the first public building finished and Studio 804 is a unique story they filmed our work extensively. Conflict and tension make good television but do not make for a good building site. Not only did their presence exacerbate problems with various community voices but it made managing the many egos and emotions of the students more difficult. For these projects to happen the students are pushed harder than they expect and achieve more than they probably honestly thought possible. Inevitably there will be times when everyone is sick of each other. During a typical year the students and I can work through these periods in a predictable fashion and it is generally kept in house. Having it filmed by someone looking to expose these moments for entertainment complicated this process and caused problems to linger longer than necessary.

547 ARTS CENTER COMMISSION

A group of citizens who were long-time supporters of the regional arts started what became the 547 Arts Center Commission and it was decided that we would build an art's center for them. Even though we were happy to have the chance to design an art gallery it seemed there were many other areas where our efforts could be productive. As the building program evolved we tried to answer a short-term need – a community meeting space – as well as long term. Once the recovery was well under way the building would become the art gallery the commission envisioned.

The art's commission helped shepherd the project through the city process but made it clear from the beginning that procuring the funding was up to us. The commission did buy the properties that became the building site, but we had to do the leg work necessary to stitch the four individually owned properties into a buildable whole – even to the point of having students visit one of the property owners in jail to have him sign the necessary paperwork. The commission was so happy to see the project happening they gave us nearly full design freedom and even allowed the early proposals to be delivered over the phone without seeing the images. In late December, the city approved the project and work could continue.

The funding for the project was still a mystery so the students started working the phones trying to raise money from those who wished to support the rebuilding effort in Greensburg, sustainable design and the educational mission of Studio 804. We received $100,000 from Google to support the program from which funds could be used to directly impact the Greensburg effort or to expand the program goals and broaden the mission of Studio 804. We also received $50,000 from the American Institute of Architects (AIA) and $50,000 loan from the Kansas Housing Commission. I saw this money as contributions to Studio 804 to use for the building of the art's center. Unfortunately, some in the town thought the money should go to Greensburg first. The group Greensburg GreenTown felt they should not only be managing the money but the building of the project itself. Studio 804 would not be able to work under this sort of arrangement. BNIM architects from Kansas City were preparing the master plan for rebuilding Greensburg and were working regularly with the leaders of Greensburg. They assured me Greensburg GreenTown was over-reaching and to proceed as planned.

Despite many concerns, we started the project working on good faith that the money issues and power plays would all be satisfactorily resolved. There was not time to wait, if this project was to be completed by the 2008 class who had done so much work to make it happen.

Since the arts center was neither a publicly funded city building nor 4,000 square feet in size it was not required to meet the LEED standards for sustainable design that the city had set2. We still wanted to live up to these standards, but I had serious doubts about adding another layer of complication to a project already on a tight schedule and more ambitious than our previous houses. Two students were LEED accredited and volunteered to take charge of this process. They wanted to build a prototype for the future development in Greensburg. I decided to pursue LEED but

only if it was going to be fully embraced and done right. We started targeting a LEED Platinum Certification from the beginning.

THE DESIGN

The building is a simple shoe box divided by the entry cross axis at about the 1/3rd point. The larger portion to the right of the entry houses a conference room and a gallery which can be used to display art or with temporary chairs become a meeting hall. The smaller portion includes the rest rooms, an office and a small kitchen that can be used to support events. Adjacent to the kitchen is a staircase leading to a large basement that can be used for storage and holds the building's mechanical systems.

For a community meeting hall and an art gallery to coexist in the same small building and to use passive sustainable strategies meant that there were some inherent incompatibilities to overcome. Foremost, was the desire to have a building that would open to the town and to the southern sun while protecting the art from the sun's UV rays - not only to keep the art from being damaged but to make for a comfortable viewing environment. The final design solution allows gatherings to spill through a set of high performance sliding glass doors onto the expansive buffalo grass lawn to the south. A four-inch concrete slab was poured on the floor frame that spans the basement and would acts as a solar mass warmed by the winter sun that enters the large south exposure. This passive heat gain combined with a geo-thermal ground source heat pump keeps the building's winter heating demands minimal.

The sliding glass doors are coated with a UV film to protect the contents of the building from the sun's damaging rays, but more was needed to allow the occupants to control heat gain as well as have the option to darken the space for presentations or open it for parties - especially in the evening. The key to this was to find a flexible, easily operated, manually controllable way to open and close the south wall. After discussing many options, we ended up in contact with a supplier of airplane hangar doors. They were interested in seeing their product used in a new way and we were interested in the possibility of having one large door that would open at the push of a button. They supplied the mechanisms to assure it would work and we designed the door. Its steel frame creates louvres calculated to shade the sun during the hotter months.

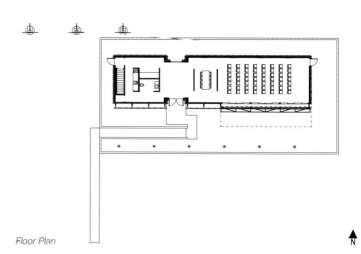

Floor Plan

N

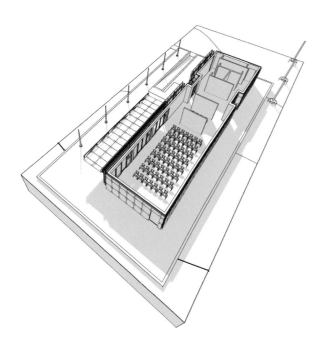

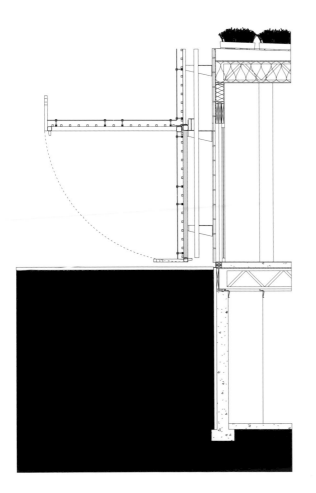

L The hydraulics of the door are strong enough to support the weight of its steel frame as well as a flush and consistently sized elevation of glass that spans across the opening. When the door is closed its presence in the composition of the south elevation is subtle. The steel frame of the door is barely visible but works as louvres to control the sun. When it is open, the door becomes a large awning that not only shades the interior but becomes a generous gesture to the lawn and the rest of Greensburg.

547 ARTS CENTER, 2008

O P

O P *To create a successful community living room, I felt it was important to set the building apart from the surrounding landscape and streets. We decided to spend the money and time to build a plinth for the building to rest upon. It not only adds to the arts center's presence, but it gives the lawn boundaries strengthening the sense of an outdoor room. The plinth walls are at seating height so they become permanent furniture. The space is used for all types of community events including projecting movies against the side of the building.*

547 ARTS CENTER, 2008

Q R S

T

Q The building has a multiple layer cladding system. The moisture barrier is part of a rainscreen with the exposed siding being horizontally run douglas fir that had been salvaged from the Sunflower Ammunition Plant near Kansas City. An unistrut frame holds a glass skin away from the wood siding. The tempered glass panels are coated with a UV filtering film and protect the wood from the sun's damage while also screening the insulated walls from the persistent Kansas winds.

R S T Green roof containers filled with sedums sit on the white single ply membrane roofing. They capture storm water and help keep the roof cool. The sedums were chosen to survive in this part of Kansas with minimal intervention. Any water that is not absorbed on the roof is directed to a cistern and is used to irrigate the site and flush the toilets. The roof hosts an array of photovoltaics that work with the wind turbines to produce 44 percent of the building's energy needs.

U V

PRODUCTION

The Sunflower Ammunition plant was a 9,000-plus acre complex with 3,000 buildings in De Soto Kansas, west of Kansas City, built on the fly starting in 1942 to immediately manufacture bomb components. During World War II as many as 12,000 people were working on site, but when the war ended the facility soon went on stand-by. It was brought back into production for a short period in the 1990s but afterward the federal government started looking for a buyer for the property and began to clear the site by burning hundreds of contaminated buildings through the early 2000's. It was part of the army's $100 million plus effort to clean the site of its environmental nightmare of explosives, arsenic, mercury and lead. There were attempts to develop the property into a Land of Oz theme park, but the plan was contingent on the US Army spending an estimated $100 million more on site clean up[6].

During the summer of 2006 one of the developers contacted Dean John Gaunt to see if the School of Architecture and Design would have any interest in salvaging some of the material.

When Studio 804 started working on the design for Greensburg I felt it would be poetic to recycle building materials from a project dedicated to warfare and use them in a new building to house the arts and become a prototype for a more sustainable way to build and live. These lofty goals did not assure a peaceful process when it came time to remove the materials. Soon we were negotiating battles on two fronts. In Greensburg, we were trying to get the city to help fund the work on our tight schedule while in De Soto, Kansas we were trying to finalize the necessary permission to dismantle a former magazine building so we could use the salvaged material as siding for the 547 Art's Center.

The contractors on site at Sunflower Ammunition who were

directing the cleanup were agreeable to helping us help Greensburg but the US Army lawyers in New Orleans were much less agreeable to having students - or anyone else the army might be liable for - on site. The more they resisted the harder the students pushed back. Finally, we were presented with a large stack of papers to sign and had to attend a training session about the toxins on site. Once these were completed we could start demolition under a constant military escort for a period of three days.

There were assurances that the building being demolished was environmentally clean but there was no guarantee about the path to the building. Every morning and each evening we were part of a motorcade led by a security detail to and from the demolition site. While dismantling the building, there was continuous supervision and the students had to stay together - always. If anyone broke the rules in any manner the entire effort would be shut down immediately.

To achieve the LEED goals only one wind turbine was needed but I felt that one turbine looked lonely against the large Kansas sky. Two turbines looked like a lonely pair. Three turbines finished the overall composition, creating a vertical balance to the horizontal shoe box resting on the wide plinth.

6) The Kansas City Star, "A look back at Sunflower Ordnance." 27 August 2013.

V *For years, I had driven the highway between Lawrence and Kansas City and had seen the Sunflower Ammunition Plant water towers on the landscape. In 2006 when Dean Gaunt presented the opportunity to visit the site and see if we could salvage any of the materials I was quick to agree. After visiting the site Rockhill and Associates did an early design for what would eventually be The Forum at Marvin Hall using several of these materials as well as planning to refurbish some of the 1940s light fixtures. It was not yet time for The Forum to happen, but the effort did plant the idea of using Sunflower's materials in my mind.*

WAREHOUSE AND PREFABRICATION

To add to what was easily becoming the most complicated Studio 804 project I did not yet have a warehouse in which to prefabricate the project. The warehouse we had been working in was undergoing a rehabilitation and was no longer available. Eventually, I found a warehouse in an abandoned nitrogen fertilizer production plant on the outskirts of Lawrence. It was not an ideal work environment. It had no heat or toilets and if not for the fact that it kept rain and snow off us it the would have been more comfortable working outside on most days. Since there were no lights Studio 804 "borrowed" a stack of lights from one of the buildings at Sunflower. They were wired up, everyone dressed warm and we started building.

After building Mod 1 through Mod 4 for the Kansas City projects I had a good understanding of the prefabrication process. I knew the limits to the bay sizes for transportation, how to handle the units and how to design them so they could be stitched together relatively easily. Even though this design was not a house it was a very similar process to what had been done before. The only real difference was the distance the units would travel. The sites in Kansas City were only about 40 miles from Lawrence while Greensburg was 270. The route dictated by the Kansas Department of Transportation added many more miles and took nearly ten hours to navigate.

Due to the time limitation and travel coordination the foundation and its excavation work had to be sub contracted to a regional company. The units were to be moved to Greensburg and set on the finished foundation the next day. Unfortunately, when the units arrived it was discovered that the top of foundation walls were significantly out of level. It might have been acceptable for a typical stick-built house or an outbuilding but not for these prefabricated units which had to be accurately set to gang properly and meet the design and performance standards of the project.

The crane was already on site and ready to go the next morning and it was not affordable to have a crane and its operator - as well as the trucks and their drivers - stay in Greensburg any longer than the one night they had scheduled. This meant the units had to be ready to set the next morning. We spent our first night in Greensburg working under lights using diamond tipped grinders to level the top of the foundation to meet the design specifications.

547 ARTS CENTER, 2008

WORKING IN GREENSBURG

Working in the wasteland created by a tornado had many problems that could be predicted along with many that could not. The problems with lodging were expected. I stayed in a hotel in Pratt, Kansas and the students stayed in a dormitory at the local community college - both were more than a half hour drive from the building site. Also anticipated, were the long drives each morning and night as well as the communications problems and difficulties buying supplies. What I did not fully understand until we were on site were the problems created by a scrambled landscape. Old storm cellars and wells were like land mines that the tornado had hidden.

Another issue that turned out to be more of a challenge than expected was the wind. Anyone who has lived and worked on the Kansas plains knows that the wind is a constant presence and we have become used to adapting. What we were not prepared for was how much dust and debris would constantly be in the air when an already arid landscape had been stripped of vegetation and covered with debris. We felt like we were constantly being sandblasted which not only made the work miserable but it was damaging our building. When the green roof containers were first set, we found that the constant wind driven debris was destroying them. There was not time to maintain the roof during construction and I knew it would be less of a problem once the site was sodded and the town cleanup was further along. It was decided to remove the roof containers and protect them from the wind by placing them in an adjacent depression where a foundation had been. This kept them out of the wind, but when a monsoon rain came through we discovered that the entire intersection drained into this excavation. Soon we were saving the plants from drowning in the pond that was created.

W Z
X Y

X When the foundation concrete was being poured one of the truck drivers was confident he knew the site and could maneuver to where he was needed. This proved to be untrue when a full concrete truck settled into one of the hidden traps that had been obscured in the scrambled landscape the tornado left behind.

FINISHING THE PROJECT

The project costs were initially carried by Studio 804 for which about half were offset by donations. In a little over a year the 547 Art Center raised enough money and received enough support from foundations to pay us back what we invested in their project. We would still be waiting if we insisted upon having the money in place before we began the project. It was the first public building finished in town and became the community living room as envisioned. It was used for meetings, gatherings and even celebratory events. It was a beacon for the future "greening of Greensburg".

This project was an exhausting and difficult process but exceptionally rewarding. Studio 804 was part of a profound effort by the people of Greensburg and the State of Kansas. It also proved that Studio 804 could take on the demands of a commercial building and the LEED process and not only succeed but flourish.

DOE STUDY

During 2010-11 The DOE ran a survey of the performance of 13 of Greensburg's "green" buildings. They found that the 547 Arts Center was producing 44 percent of the energy it used and was saving 70 percent in energy costs when compared to the typical building of its type. The components they choose to highlight in the buildings' success were the daylighting levels, the well-insulated and sealed envelope, the three wind turbines, the photovoltaics on the roof and ground source heat pump for heating and cooling[7].

7) United States Department of Energy, "Rebuilding it Better: Greensburg, Kansas High Performance Buildings Meeting Energy Savings Goals." pp 3-4.

547 ARTS CENTER, 2008

07

THE KANSAS CITY SUSTAINABLE HOUSES

After finishing the LEED Platinum certified 547 Arts Center in Greensburg, Kansas I wanted to make sustainable design a greater emphasis in the work of Studio 804. I wanted to research and implement the types of technologies I felt the students needed to understand to be part of the changes that were occurring in architecture to address the problems of climate change.

These projects are LEED Platinum designs that minimize energy use and use photovoltaics and wind turbines to generate much of the power they need to operate. This is also when we begin to work to the PHIUS (Passive House Institute US) standards which led to a complete re-evaluation of how we build and how the use of technology and passive natural systems can be manipulated.

3716 SPRINGFIELD STREET HOUSE, 2009

Rosedale Neighborhood, Kansas City, Kansas
LEED Platinum Certified

OUR FIRST SPECULATIVE PROJECT

After the success of the Mod houses and the 547 Arts Center Studio 804 had managed to save enough money to develop our own project. I had been hoping to get to this point for a few years now. I knew the added freedom that came with doing speculative work would be worth the increased risk. The dependence on others to generate work had been one of the more stressful parts of running the program, especially as my educational and architectural goals were becoming more experimental with an eye toward the future of how we are going build. The housing authorities in Kansas City had been exceptionally supportive but asking them to take larger risks on houses that were increasingly out of the mainstream of American housing would be more than I could reasonably expect. Especially in the buyers' market that had existed since the burst of the housing bubble. That is assuming the buyers could get the funds they needed as the banks were severely cutting back on mortgage loans as this was a primary source of the bank failures.

I had a class of students arriving in August and they had signed up for a comprehensive building experience so I decided to try to find a way to create something unique that would create a demand despite the current market. We found a piece of property, funded the construction and again hoped to tap in to the interest in living more centralized lives in urban centers. But this time, rather than focusing chiefly on affordable housing for first time buyers I wanted to continue what we had started in Greensburg. We choose to not only aggressively pursue LEED Platinum certification, but we also wanted to experiment with the sustainable technologies and building techniques that would allow us to create a house that was fully energy self-sufficient as well as built with as healthy and resource neutral materials as possible.

This meant we were going to be building a higher cost house than the Mod years and it would require changes to how we designed and approached construction. When it was time to put the house on the market these new goals would exacerbate that already familiar problem of getting a fair appraisal to allow a potential buyer to get an adequate mortgage loan. The appraisers' formulas were not going to give us substantial credit for the innovative sustainable features and high-quality construction. There are checklists for amenities, but not for PVs, wind turbines, geo-thermal wells, exceptionally high insulation values and high-performance windows. It is essentially as if these things do not exist. We would have to build a large enough house with enough square-footage, bedrooms, bathrooms and typical amenities to offset the cost of the sustainable ones in an appraisal. Either that, or we would have to find someone with the cash at hand to buy it without a loan.

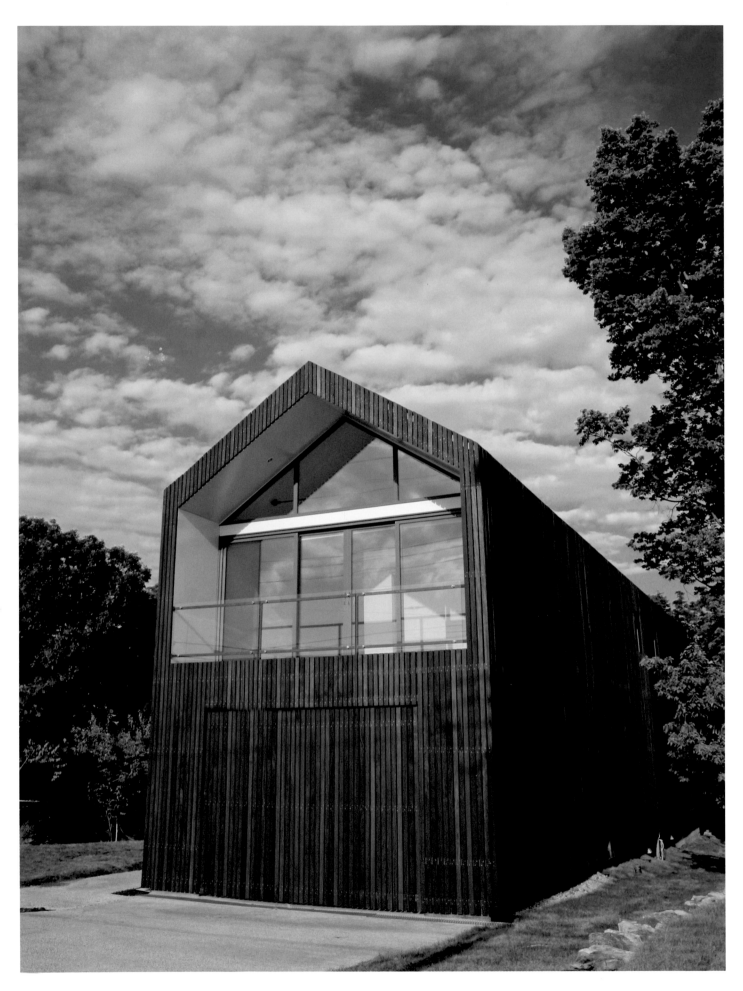

BUILDING STRATEGY

To build a building this large and advanced as prefabricated units in Lawrence would be difficult, if not impossible. The program was for a high performance four-bedroom house that would fit on its narrow site, stay within the setbacks and meet the pervious vs. non-pervious site surface requirements. It was inevitable that it would be a two-story solution with a high premium on quality construction and an air tight envelope.

This was to be our project from beginning to end. I wanted the students on site every day doing the excavation, building the formwork for the foundation and working with the subcontractors who were drilling the geo-thermal wells. This independence gave us the freedom to explore and try things that others would not want to risk. I was still concerned about the students driving from Lawrence to Kansas City every day so we rented long term rooms that allowed them to stay in Kansas City when they wanted to. Each student could stay or go each night. This gave them the flexibility then needed to operate in Lawrence and Kansas City but cut down on unnecessary drives and lessened the daily concerns about dark, busy, snow or ice packed roads.

NET METERING

Codes do not allow a technically "off grid" building in Kansas City, but we approached the design as if they did. We did not want to add to the expense and complications that come with a bank of batteries like we used in Greensburg when we knew this was no longer necessary if we could get the cooperation we needed. We lobbied the local utility supplier to provide net metering so the owners would be credited during the periods the house generates excess energy. Then they could draw from these credits during periods the conditions were not advantageous. When the house was finished, it was not only the first LEED Platinum certified house in the Kansas City metropolitan area but it was also the first building in Wyandotte County to use net metering. It was past time for all communities in America to offer this option and it was a valuable experience for the students to play a role in breaking down this barrier in at least this one community.

COMPREHENSIVE SUSTAINABLE DESIGN

This project is another addition to the revitalization of the Rosedale neighborhood in Kansas City, Kansas. Like the Mods it is near the University of Kansas Medical Center, nestled on a relatively secluded site with a broad exposure to the southern sun. It takes advantage of its orientation for solar heat gain as well as capturing the prevailing breezes to cool the house. It acts as solar chimney bringing fresh air in through low operable windows on the south elevation which rises as it warms and vents out operable skylights on the second floor. These are the types of strategies we have always used and have been used in vernacular architecture for generations. What was unique on this house was the comprehensive sustainable choices that were part of every building feature from finishes to the ground cover.

We used high-performance glazing with insulated fiberglass frames as well as radiant floor heat to supplement the passive solar heat and the geo-thermal heat pump system. This was the first project to use an energy-recovery ventilator to capture, filter and reuse the heat generated by daily living in the house. We did everything in our means to aggressively minimize the energy loads over the year and offset it with integrated active systems. The house is powered by a 4.8-kilowatt photovoltaic array and a vertical axis wind turbine, the target for the combined energy production was calculated by taking 70 percent of the total wattage that the house would use with all electrical devices in operation at the same time. Admittedly, the wind turbine does very little in comparison to the PV, but it's an icon in the neighborhood. It says a lot about the intent of the house and beliefs of the owner and we loved the way it looks. Sometimes even energy strategies are more than numbers and formulas. Sometimes the final choices are as poetic as they are functional.

The sustainable strategies did not end with energy efficiency. We also used low-flow valve plumbing fixtures, all the materials, paints, flooring, sealants and adhesives used inside the house emit low or no volatile organic compounds. The entire site was planted with a drought-resistant fescue. It is a sod that is highly recommended in Kansas as a replacement for conventional turf. All hardscape surfaces surrounding the exterior of the house are porous to allow the storm water to seep into the subsurface. This includes the use of pervious concrete for the driveway.

One of the most notable features is the cumaru wood rain-screen cladding. It was a progression from what we had done on the earlier Mod houses by extending the rainscreen over the roof and even cladding the garage door to give the building skin a uniform appearance. Integral gutters and downspouts are hidden behind the rain-screen and carry rainwater to an underground cistern.

A	E
B	
C	
D	

D *Three geo-thermal wells were drilled to use the consistent temperature of the earth to assist the heat pump in heating and cooling the building.*

E *The concrete mix included 30 percent fly ash, a by-product of the coal industry, it can be used as a substitute for a percentage of the cement and its high embodied energy.*

G *The vertical application of the FSC certified tropical cumaru wood rainscreen wraps the entire exterior of the residence to create a "cover" of sorts. The gutters and downspouts are hidden; the 24 photovoltaic panels are flush with the Cumaru rainscreen on the south slope of the gable. The garage door is visually part of the screen and not immediately recognizable. All the cumaru is finished with Penofin, a penetrating oil, to bring out its color and improve its durability.*

F G

THE DESIGN

The house's barn-inspired design conforms to the neighborhood while updating the classic gable with clean lines and large expanses of glazing. Everything is streamlined including the PVs on the roof that are set flush with the wood rainscreen to retain the clean lines of the building's form.

It is a 2,500 square-foot, four-bedroom, two-and-a-half bath residence that gives the owner plenty of space for a variety of living arrangements while minimizing the ecological footprint of their lives. A glass enclosed stair tower divides the building and anchors the design. On the first floor, the stairs separate the open plan of the galley kitchen, dining room, and living areas from the utility spaces such as the half bath and the one car garage. It also is the access to the full basement where there is a laundry room and ample storage located around the advanced mechanical systems. On the Second Floor the stair tower rests between a loft space that looks over the living room and a generous master bedroom suite that features a custom designed bathroom and a walk out balcony with views of the 39th street corridor.

The living spaces and the loft open to the site through a two-floor glazed wall that makes up the entire west elevation. It extends views to a wooded preserve that butts to the property line and is protected from future residential or commercial development. The first floor opens to the south through the louvred glass wall that allows for passive solar gain and has operable windows for ventilation. Daylight floods the spaces when desired but can be controlled with sun screens.

We could not immediately sell the house, but we did rent it to help balance the books until we finally did. It sold for about half what I estimated its real value to be, but it was enough to cover the cost of materials and help fund our next project.

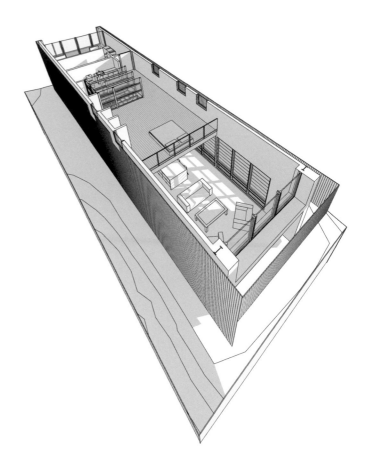

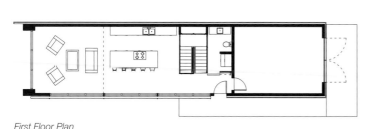

First Floor Plan

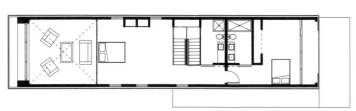

Second Floor Plan

H *FSC certified Jatoba hardwood flooring is featured in the upstairs loft and bedroom spaces and continues over the edge of the loft to wrap the kitchen ceiling to and create a visual link between the spaces.*

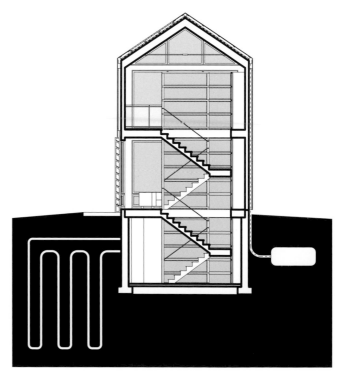

I J K
L M

I To create the fully glazed end wall we had to find an engineered alternative to the typical braced wall framing requirements. We designed a steel moment frame that resists the lateral loads and allows us the openness we wanted.

J K The epoxy coated concrete floors provides thermal mass for the passive heating and cooling. It also encases the tubes for the radiant heating system. Radiant heat creates a feeling of warmth at much lower temperatures than forced air because there is much less air movement.

L Engineered lumber was used to frame the house. Each framing member was precisely measured and cut to achieve a collective waste factor of only 4.37 percent.

M Not unlike the Greensburg project we went back to the Sunflower Ammunition Plant and demolished a building. When we did not have to meet a code standard that prohibited it, this salvaged material was used in the framing of the building.

O   Q
———
P

P *A steel frame with glass shingles encloses the staircase and provides daylighting and spatial separation between the front rooms and the back of the house. Night time lighting is supplied with a low-voltage cable system.*

PRESCOTT PASSIVE HOUSE, 2010

Prescott Neighborhood, Kansas City, Kansas
LEED Platinum Certified
Passive House Institute US Certified (PHIUS)

AFFORDABLE AND SUSTAINABLE

With the house on Springfield Street I had finally broken through the financial barrier that kept Studio 804 from developing our own projects and I was not going to willingly turn back. The Springfield Street house was yet to sell when the class of 2010 was gathering. I was renting it to cover some of the costs. I was still able to piece together the funds we needed to get started on a new speculative house. This time we were building in the Prescott neighborhood in Kansas City. Another fine old Wyandotte County, Kansas neighborhood that was trying to dig itself out of years of decline. The neighborhood association was supportive when we approached them about building a new and unique house on one of their streets lined with early 20th century homes.

I planned to target a different buyer with this project so that it might more easily sell, while not directly competing with the Springfield Street house which was still on the market. The Springfield house had been largely about achieving LEED Platinum certification and aggressively pursuing sustainable technology and building techniques. It was a bout performance more than budget. I had hoped it would be justified once we sold the property which only ended up being about half true, but I knew the risks of building a unique and advanced home in a marginal neighborhood. For the Prescott house, partly out of a sense of responsibility as an educator of socially aware young minds, but also out of necessity, I wanted to see if we could address affordability without abandoning these ecological concerns. Unfortunately, these are often conflicting goals. Many of the sustainable energy strategies require high-efficiency mechanical systems and on site active energy generation, all with high up-front costs. We chose to do as much as we could to promote sustainability while reaching out to the low-income family buyer. The Department of Housing and Urban Development considers low income to be a family earning less the 80 percent of the area medium income (AMI) and affordability means that the housing costs will not exceed 30 percent of that income. We sought to build a sustainable house that could be purchased while living under these constraints.

PASSIVE HOUSE INSTITUTE US (PHIUS)

I still intended to pursue LEED Platinum Certification. Now I knew the process and felt that much of what it requires should be common practice anyway - even for low income housing - and we wanted to show it was possible. To do this for a self-imposed tight budget meant we had to be creative in how we would address the subject of energy use for heating and cooling. We would have to do it passively, with intelligent design and a high-quality envelope. We would not be able to use pho-

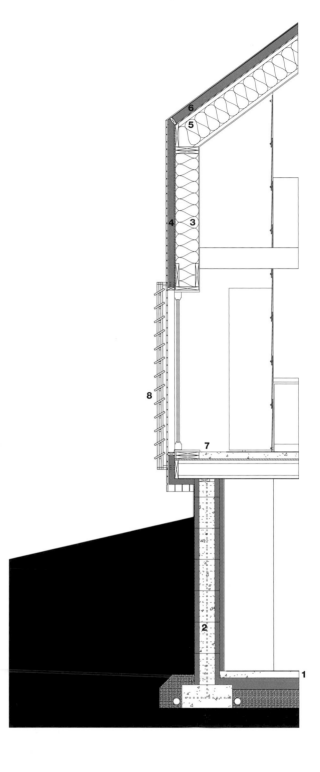

A E
B C
D
       F G

A D *To achieve the insulation levels required of a PHIUS certified building we had to have exceptionally thick walls. We used engineered lumber I-joists and LVLs throughout. The cavities between were packed with cellulose fiber insulation. Then three more inches of rigid board insulation was added to the outside of the walls to reach our R-value goals.*

B C *Our Prescott neighbors were very supportive of the project which showed itself in many ways including a local resident who made tamales and sold them to us on a regular basis despite the language barrier between us. It was one of the highlights of the project for me and the students*

E *Detail Section:*
1) 9" XPS Insulation

2) ICF Basement Walls
3) 12" Engineered Lumber Framing
4) 3" XPS Insulation Board
5) 16" Engineer Lumber Framing
6) 5" Polyiso Insulation Panels
7) 4" Concrete Thermal Mass Floor
8) Calculated Sun Control Louvres

F G *As the process became more common in the United State we started working with third parties to do the blower door test and document the results. At this time however, we had to purchase the equipment and do the tests ourselves. PHIUS provided us with software necessary to determine the required performance of the building and document the test results. We then used this information for our submittal for certification.*

tovoltaics or wind turbines to offset energy use. We would not be able to afford geo-thermal wells or radiantly heated slabs to assist the primary mechanical system. This inspired us to learn more about PHIUS and their certification process. They are the US arm of the German institute that supports the advancement of passive energy saving construction and certifies buildings using scientific criteria. A few years earlier I had read a piece in the New York Times about the PassivHaus movement in Europe and was intrigued. They were making claims that, if done properly, the construction techniques they promote create buildings that require little or no supplemental heating or cooling and would only cost 6 percent more than typical construction. Years later they were still rare in America, but we now had access to the certification process through PHIUS and the technology was more available and affordable.

The PassivHaus standards are analogous to building a thermos in which energy loads are drastically reduced by means of a super-insulated, virtually airtight building shell which allows as close to no heat transfer as humanly possible – "maximize your gains, minimize your losses". The Prescott Passive House was certified by meeting these five criteria.

PASSIVE HOUSE INSTITUTE US (PHIUS) DESIGN FEATURES

a) The building envelope is continuously insulated to levels that exceed the local codes by at least a multiple of three and often more. There can be no thermal bridging created by the structure or any other architectural components. This includes the basement and the slab which must be fully insulated. The common practice of insulating the perimeter is not good enough as it breaks the continuity of the "thermos".

b) The building envelope is virtually air tight, thus it prevents air infiltration and the loss of conditioned air. This was verified by blower door tests administered to PHIUS standards. There are absolutely no penetrations of the exterior envelope and all the electrical, mechanical and plumbing runs were accounted for in the floor frames and interior partitions. To assure the accuracy of the blower door test requires going to extremes such as taping the keyholes before the procedure begins.

c) The windows and doors are of the highest performance standards available, in our case triple pane assemblies with exceptionally tight weather seals. In 2010 these units were impos-

sible to purchase in the US and we had to order ours in Europe and have them shipped. This caused some scheduling concerns as we were, as always, working on a fast track schedule and have a very firm completion date. If we did not have the windows and doors when we need them to complete the building envelope the entire building time line would be hobbled. It was a constant source of concern until the day the windows were on American soil and heading our way.

d) We used balanced ventilation as opposed to a supply-only or exhaust-only system. This means there are two fans, one bringing outside air into the building, and the other exhausting stale interior air, resulting in roughly balanced airflows. In most balanced ventilation systems, heat and moisture are exchanged between the two airstreams, reducing the heating and cooling loads caused by outside ventilation air. Since the envelope is air tight, if the windows are closed this is the only source of fresh air. One of the principal selling points of a PHIUS house is that all the heat produced by day to day living - showers, cooking, exercise - is captured and used to condition this incoming fresh air. With the advanced building envelope, this can minimize or eliminate the need for supplemental heat. These systems are known as HRVs (heat recovery ventilators) and ERVs (energy recovery ventilators). HRVs only exchange heat between the airstreams, while ERVs exchange both heat and moisture. Our often humid climate required the use of an ERV. Since we have yearly temperature extremes that do not allow us to solely focus on heating or cooling we added a mini split for supplemental heating or cooling when needed. A mini split has minimal impact on the building and minimal costs since it does not require duct work.

e) The design concept works hand in glove with the passive strategies for heating, cooling and daylighting. The interior volume, with a double-height living room, allows full penetration of daylight through south-facing glass and strategically placed skylights on the north-facing slope of the roof. Louvres over the buildings south-facing windows are angled to maximize winter sunlight and minimize summer's direct sunlight to seasonally control heat gain. Cast-in-place concrete floors provide thermal mass to store the sun's heat and release it at night. During the temperate months, operable windows and skylights promote natural ventilation.

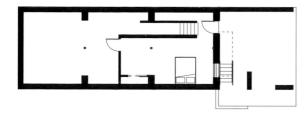

Basement Floor Plan

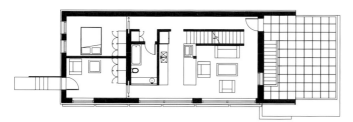

First Floor Plan

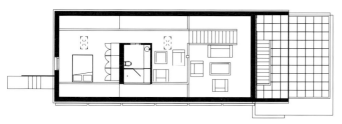

Second Floor Plan

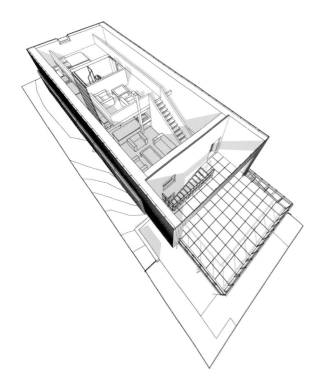

THE DESIGN

To meet the PHIUS goals and achieve our targeted 90 percent reduction in base line heating and cooling costs we had to design very deep wall and roof assemblies to hold the insulation required and to make it possible to eliminate thermal bridging. Using engineered lumber - which is manufactured from fast growing under utilized trees and milling waste - was the only viable option to use to frame the building. The wall studs are a combination of 12" wood I-joists and LVLs (laminated veneer lumber) and the roof rafters are 16" I-joists. The cavities are packed tight with cellulose insulation. The ridge beam allows for a minimum of columns to interrupt the open, daylighted interior. The walls and roof were sheathed and then an extra three inches of XPS insulation board was applied to the walls and an extra five inches of Polyiso insulation panels were added to the roof. The entire assembly was then sheathed again and wrapped in the moisture barrier that was the first layer of the rainscreen. Every joint in the sheathing and frame assemblies had to be sealed to block air infiltration. To create an insulated foundation, we used ICFs (insulated concrete forms) for the foundation and then additional insulation on the interior walls to meet PHIUS standards. We also had nine inches of XPS insulation under the slab.

Prescott Passive House is a 1,700 square-foot, three-bedroom, two-bathroom residence. Despite its modest size, the open floor plan creates a spacious interior. The site slopes steeply from the back property line down to the street. The front of the foundation is screened by a carport that extends from the front elevation and supports a large outdoor deck. The house can be entered from the carport through a basement door to a finished flex space or by taking a staircase to the deck where one can enter the living room on the main floor. The deck has expansive views of the Prescott neighborhood and the Kansas City skyline. The two-story living room is open to the kitchen and dining room. An open staircase connects to the multi-use loft at the top of the stairs and the master bedroom suite that extends to the back of the house. The bathrooms for both floors are efficiently stacked and flooded with natural light through a two-story frosted glass wall that faces the extensive glazing along the south wall of the house. Two more bedrooms are located on the first floor at the back of house behind the bathroom core.

H J K
I L

H I J K L *As is the case with any building planning to achieve LEED certification all the materials, paints, flooring, sealants and adhesives used inside the addition emit low or no volatile organic compounds.*

LEED AND PHIUS CERTIFICATION

When the Prescott Passive House finished, it was Studio 804's third consecutive LEED Platinum certified building and it was the first PHIUS certified house in Kansas and one of a handful in the US.

M	O	P
	Q	R
N	S	T

M *The students work on the pervious concrete driveway and sidewalks. Pervious concrete is an open cell pavement that allows water to pass directly through its surface into a deep gravel bed below where it is gradually absorbed by the subsurface eliminating the typical storm runoff associated with concrete slabs.*

N *The ICF foundation walls were coated with traditional three coat stucco.*

S *The air barrier was created by sealing every joint in the building frame and sheathing.*

U V
—
W

V W *In the spirit of the age-old Japanese shou-sugi-ban tradition, the exterior of the Prescott Passive House is clad in a charred Douglas fir rain screen. It is a UV- and pest resistant brown/black skin that wraps the house.*

PRESCOTT PASSIVE HOUSE, 2010

08

THE EDUCATIONAL FACILITIES

With Studio 804 I had been doing gradually more ambitious housing and this probably would have continued indefinitely if not for the world economic collapse of 2008 which caused the housing market in the United States to crater. Our previous two sustainable houses in Kansas City had been architecturally successful but had not sold which meant we had no resources to start another speculative project on our own.

The 547 Arts Center and these technologically advanced houses had proven that students could successfully complete larger more complex projects than had been previously assumed. When the University of Kansas approached me with the opportunity to design an educational building dedicated to sustainability I agreed. The resulting Center for Design Research led to more university projects – each larger and more complicated than the one before.

THE CENTER FOR DESIGN RESEARCH, 2011

The University of Kansas Campus, Lawrence, Kansas
LEED Platinum Certified
Passive House Institute US (PHIUS) Certified

CHAMNEY FARM

In 1963, the University of Kansas acquired the 130-acre tract of rolling land and the ten buildings that made up the Chamney Dairy Farm adjacent to the main campus. Harold Chamney started the farm in 1912 and it was one of the largest dairy farms in the area. By the time the family sold the property to the University of Kansas the stone house and the iconic steel-roofed barn were part of the burgeoning east/west artery that extends from the primary entrance of the University of Kansas campus to the ever-expanding development of the west side of Lawrence that had by then surrounded the farm.

The University rehabilitated the farm buildings and the School of Fine Arts used them for arts and craft studios - including a large ceramics facility and its kilns which are still located in one of the original outbuildings and in use today. By 2011, the Center for Design Research (CDR) occupied the Chamney House and there was interest in expanding the program to meet the increasing role of research to support higher education.

THE CENTER FOR DESIGN RESEARCH (CDR)

The CDR was formed to promote research but we also saw an opportunity to promote the education of not only the students at University of Kansas but the Lawrence community in sustainable strategies, material innovation and building efficiency. The CDRs research focuses on interdisciplinary collaboration in the research and development of consumer products and services. In 2011 they had finished several successful industry sponsored projects for the likes of Herman Miller, Bushnell, Nokia, and the North Kansas City Hospital. An improved facility would allow the CDR to pursue an even more ambitious agenda. They hoped to approach larger corporate entities such as Ford or Garmin as well as federal programs like the Departments of Energy and Transportation to propose collaborative efforts.

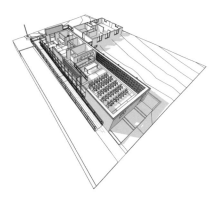

THE CENTER FOR DESIGN RESEARCH, 2011

THE CENTER FOR DESIGN RESEARCH, 2011

TROMBE WALL

A Trombe wall is a passive solar assembly named after its inventor. It is composed of two walls surrounding an enclosed air space. The inside layer is the Trombe wall made of a high mass material such as masonry or concrete and the exterior is glass. On sunny days, the mass of the Trombe wall not only absorbs the heat of the sun hitting its surface but also the heat trapped in the air space between the walls – which further heats the mass wall. It then slowly releases the stored heat into the building at night.

At the CDR, sun light passes through a butt-glazed curtain wall to heat a 30" deep air space and a ten-inch-thick Trombe wall. The wall is composed of 6-inch-thick concrete masonry units filled with sand and clad on both sides with two inches of limestone. The wall also provides shear support with steel diagonals that are enveloped by the masonry. From the exterior, the Trombe wall appears to be a continuation of the building's stone cladding but it has shifted back behind the flush face of the glass wall.

The stone of the Trombe wall matches that of the exterior cladding except that the cut stones are half the size of the exterior coursing. This allowed us to use much of the cut off waste generated in the production of the cladding. We also inserted ½" sheets of laminated glass between every fourth course. The glass extends all the way through the assembly and creates bands of light across what would otherwise be a dark interior surface. In addition to the aesthetics of this detail it creates a soft daylight for the ramp between the reception area and the multipurpose room.

For a Trombe wall to efficiently support a building with such stringent energy goals the air space either needs to be vented or the sun must be dynamically managed with active shading. Calculated fixed louvres would not control the heat gain well enough during the swing seasons to avoid over heating unless sensors could automatically vent the trapped air and bring in fresh cooler air. This would require extensive sensors and complex controls that would add design time and consultants. Also, the fixed louvres are not effective during the increasingly unseasonable weather many parts of the planet are regularly experiencing. An automated louvre system could be successfully used but they are also costly and would not be in keeping with the minimal design language.

This led us to another up and coming technology in the field of sustainable design. Sage Glass was a company developing electrochromic glass at the time. They manufacture insulated glass units that are electrically wired and when voltage is applied can change their light transmission properties to adapt to the immediate needs of the building. When the sun is being allowed to enter the space the glass appears clear, when it is blocking the heat they darken but are still transparent. Even during the hottest days there is still enough daylight passing through to minimize the need for artificial lighting. The CDR staff can also change the electrochromic tint on demand with the press of a button to temporarily darken or lighten the space as desired. By using this innovative glazing and by building our own thermally broken steel curtain wall assembly we created a south glass wall that was flush with the stone facade and unencumbered by any type of visible sun control.

SUSTAINABLE STANDARDS

Along with the features described thus far the completed building has the highly insulated, air tight envelope combined with the efficient mechanical system that is typical of a PHIUS certified building. When combined with high performance fixtures and a successful passive heating strategy the building's energy needs are greatly offset by the wind turbine and the 32 photovoltaic panels on the roof. When these features are joined with the typical LEED features such as a green roof, water harvesting, low VOC finishes as well as first electric vehicle charging station in Kansas gracing the parking lot you end up with a building that was recognized by the Swiss Holcim Foundation with an Award for sustainable design.

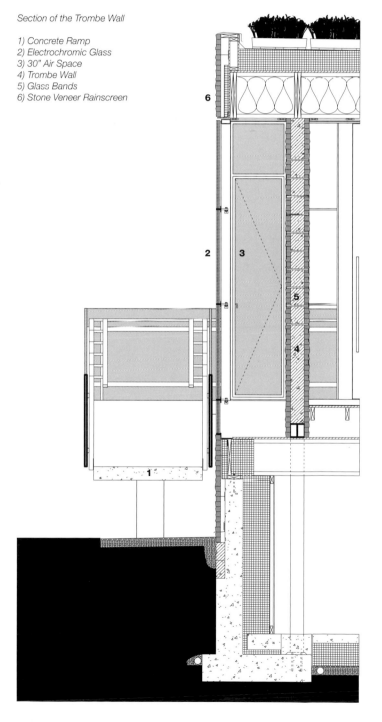

Section of the Trombe Wall

1) Concrete Ramp
2) Electrochromic Glass
3) 30" Air Space
4) Trombe Wall
5) Glass Bands
6) Stone Veneer Rainscreen

THE CENTER FOR DESIGN RESEARCH, 2011

THE CENTER FOR DESIGN RESEARCH, 2011

INDUSTRY SUPPORT

By exploring provocative ideas in sustainable design Studio 804 can attract building industry support. This cooperation makes these projects possible within limited budgets. The companies are given the opportunity to work with the latest sustainable design standards and techniques. This helps them to educate themselves and train their employees as well as being a valuable marketing tool when the building is finished and garners recognition.

When the design of the CDR began, there were less than a dozen PHIUS certified buildings in North America (including Studio 804's Prescott Passive House) and there were no certified commercial buildings. There were several companies that wanted the opportunity to be part of a PHIUS certified building, let alone the first commercial example in the US, so they were willing to negotiate friendly terms to do so.

A	B	
	C	D

C Electrochromic insulated glass units use multiple layers of ceramic film that automatically change their relationship to one another when electrically charged to tint the glass and control the amount of the sun's heat and light that passes through. By using GPS, a central computer has access to real time weather information at the site and can alter the glass to control how much of the sun's heat and light is entering the rooms and how much is entering the Trombe wall assembly.

E G
—
F

E F G *The ERV intake and exhaust are framed by the downspouts which are enclosed in glass. LEDs are located inside each and the vertical bands of light create shadows across the face of the stone highlighting the qualities of the coursing.*

THE CENTER FOR DESIGN RESEARCH, 2011

GALILEO'S PAVILION, 2012

Johnson County Community College Campus,
Overland Park, Kansas
LEED Platinum Certified

A CDR FOR JCCC

While finishing the Center for Design Research (CDR) during the summer of 2011 the director of sustainability from Johnson County Community College (JCCC) approached me about doing something similar on their campus. JCCC's strategic plan calls for the college to champion environmental sustainability in curriculum and in the college's infrastructure, transforming the physical campus into a living learning laboratory[1].

No project had yet been chosen for the 2012 class, so I agreed to meet with the representatives of JCCC and see if a project could be developed in the necessary time period. By this time Studio 804 often developed our own projects which affords us the freedom to experiment in design and technology but to also have control over the schedule and budget. When building for a client there is not only the potential loss of design freedom, but the work must be done to a specific budget and scheduling becomes more complicated. To design and build a building of such significance in a single school year means the work often must diverge from typical building delivery procedures. It was tough to embrace being embroiled in another complex bureaucratic process where so much of my time and that of the students is spent on issues that have little to do with the quality of the architecture. It was difficult enough on the CDR building which was for our home university where we had built in support.

The concerns were lessened upon learning that JCCC is an autonomous island in the city of Overland Park in Johnson County, Kansas. Any development built on campus has only to negotiate with the college for approvals and permits. They hire a third-party inspector to run their inspection process. This streamlined approach and the opportunity to expand on the sustainable strategies explored in the CDR eventually led me to decide this project was worth the challenges and risks.

We ended up making a proposal for a $750,000 project that would include two new classrooms and explore both traditional and new concepts in sustainable building design. The goal was to create an inspiring space for learning that would also serve as an information center for the campus and the community at large by displaying how the built environment can be responsibly developed in the future by combining common sense strategies and emerging technologies.

JCCC is in the Kansas City metropolitan area. The campus has been built over the last 45 years and has a business park vibe with its nondescript brick buildings and large parking lots. But,

1) JCCC's sustainability mission is detailed on their website at: http://www.jccc.edu/about/campus/sustainability.html

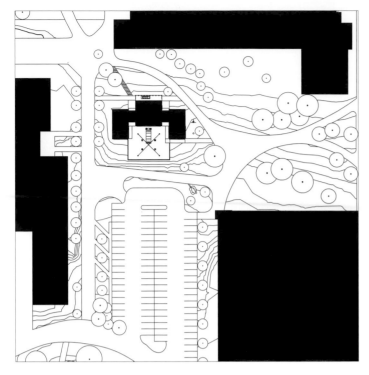

Site Plan

with increasing interest in sustainable design and the striking Nerman Museum of Contemporary Art designed by Kyu Sung Woo Architects Inc. which opened in 2007 the college's architectural goals were clearly changing. Today, it is one of the most successful community college's in the country with robust enrollment and outstanding curriculum offerings.

CHOOSING A LOCATION ON CAMPUS

Initially, the college offered us locations on the perimeter of the campus where most of the new development was occurring. I felt that JCCC's mission would be better served if the building was more centrally located. As I toured campus I was drawn to the location of a landscape sculpture named Galileo's Garden. It was near the student union at the heart of campus in a quad that simply served as circulation. There was not a significant building facing it t o give it a presence on campus. I envisioned this ill-defined greenspace becoming a pedestrian hub and a node of student activity and social interaction. I also felt that Galileo's Garden was an interesting parallel to what Studio 804 was trying to achieve and that the sculpture would be an even stronger work of art if it were given a framed space by a new building that shared the same vision.

The choice of the site - though it proved appropriate for the project - did lead to some difficulties. The original utility lines at JCCC were installed about 40 years earlier and the college only had general knowledge of their location. We started work under the impression that the chosen site was clear of easements. During construction, it was discovered that the building was going to be eight feet from a water main and that the utility easement agreement with the water district was for ten feet of clearance. We also learned that there would be $25,000 tap fee to access the water. This is not common and in the rush to get started this information was not gathered. Once all the facts were ascertained it was clear that either the building or the water main had to move two feet. The University refused to help with these surprises and it was the first sign that there would be little give and take with JCCC when discussing money. It was not a good start to the project as it caused delays the schedule could not afford and stressed an already maximized budget.

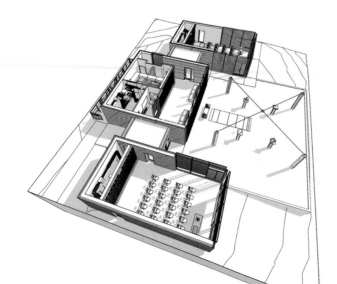

A B

C D

A SIMPLE PLAN AND FORM

I tried to keep the design work as democratic and collaborative as possible but after the experience with the CDR and the schedule demand for this project I did actively steer the design of Galileo's Pavilion. I insisted that the forms be kept simple and the student efforts be directed toward design development and innovation. The U-shaped layout creates a south opening public courtyard that wraps Galileo's Garden. I felt the building should create a backdrop for the sculpture and that it was to have a quiet but highly refined envelope. As with CDR there was a short period of dissent by some in the class but also like CDR they were quickly convinced there was still much design work to be done.

In December of 2011 the proposal was presented to the JCCC Board of Directors and we were given permission to proceed. The plan had two classrooms in each arm of the U connected by a lounge. It would be a gathering space for students and an educational platform for sustainability. The project was funded by JCCC using a portion of the sustainability fees that are part of each student's tuition. The JCCC students were represented in the building process by the Student Sustainability Committee who was kept informed as the project progressed.

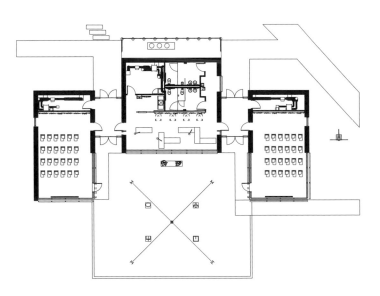

Floor Plan

C D *Galileo's Garden, was commissioned by JCCC in 1984 and created by renowned Kansas City artist Dale Eldred (American, 1933 -1993). It is a painted steel sculpture that works with the sun's seasonal and daily cycles to function as a timepiece and honor the spirit of Galileo Galilei. Suspended on steel cables at the center of Eldred's work is a stainless-steel disk with a hole in its center. On the ground beneath the disk is a nickel-coated plate etched with lines that denote the 21st day of each month. As the sun passes overhead, the disk casts a shadow on the lines, providing a solar calendar. The sculptural elements on the four pedestals represent an equatorial dial, polar sundial, latitude finder and equatorial sundial and were tools Galileo would have used to measure the position of the sun at different times as he investigated his controversial theory that the earth revolved around the sun.*

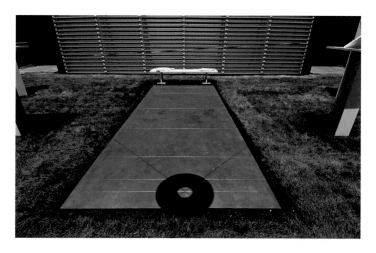

GALILEO'S PAVILION

Galileo's Pavilion and Eldred's sculpture Galileo's Garden share the mission of raising awareness about the cycles of nature and how they interact with the built environment. The design does this in many ways that range from taking advantage of the daily sun angles to the use of new technologies to assure the building's mechanical system functions as efficiently as possible.

The division between interior and exterior was dematerialized with a strong interplay between the two. The classrooms, and student lounge are not only visually open to the courtyard and Galileo's Garden through floor to ceiling glass walls but employ passive solar design strategies to help keep the spaces heated and cooled. Exterior frosted glass louvres are calculated to block out the intense summer sun while allowing the lower winter sun to penetrate the rooms, heating the thermal mass of the concrete floor and then radiating the heat into the space at night. The glass louvres are opaque enough to block the sun's heat but still allow enough light to pass through to create soft, consistent daylighting that will lessen the need for energy to operate artificial lighting. During warm weather the concrete floors remain shaded and cool and when the weather is nice operable windows are strategically placed to capture the prevailing winds and cross ventilate through opposite side windows or operable skylights. The skylights also provide crucial natural light to over 60 feet of living green walls that create striking backdrops for the classrooms and lounge while also filtering toxins from the air and acting as sound absorbers.

The energy load is also reduced through the coordination of all the various building systems. Occupancy sensors assure the space coordinates with the daily fluctuations in use. The Variable Refrigerant Flow (VRF) system allows for simultaneous heating and cooling of all the spaces as may be needed in a building used for assembly. To assure that the conditioned air is used efficiently the structural frame of Galileo's Pavilion is over three times as thick as conventional framing which allows more insulation to be used between the structural components. All the construction joints were caulked or foamed and the entire assembly was pressure tested to assure its tightness. Six inches of rigid insulation board were placed beneath the basement slab and 12 inches were installed on the inside of the foundation walls. All the joints between the insulation boards were sealed with a barrier wrap to assure an airtight crawl space. The result is a building envelope that is insulated to values four times those done by conventional methods.

The common sense passive design features coupled with the advanced mechanical system and high-performance envelope not only provide efficient heating and cooling but also reduce the operating costs and extend the life of the building. With these strategies in place the use of photovoltaic (PV) panels and a wind turbine succeeded in producing the targeted 70 percent of the building's energy needs over a calendar year. Net metering enables the college to be credited for excess energy production during peak hours of sun and wind and use these credits during less productive times. To support the building's educational role an energy management system displays the building's real-time energy use and production on a monitor in the lounge. This allows the building's users to immediately see the impact of the photovoltaics and the wind turbine on the building's overall energy use.

GALILEO'S PAVILION, 2012

MATERIALS

The materials for both the structure and the finishes at Galileo's Pavilion were carefully chosen to reduce the use of natural resources and the emissions of volatile organic compounds (VOC's). Using recyclable materials throughout reduces the need to use landfills when the day comes that the building is no longer viable.

The facade of the building is clad with a slate panel rainscreen made from reclaimed chalk boards gathered from several demolition contractors in the Midwest who had been taking down obsolete school buildings as well as a PTA member from a school district in Iowa who had the slabs stored in her garage as she worked to sell them. We also used large insulated glass units to open the building to the courtyard that were originally part of the West Edge project which was a failed development slated for the Country Club Plaza in Kansas City. The glass units were already assembled when the work stopped and were available to us in the secondary building material market. We started the building design with their sizes in mind.

E G
F H

G H *All the lighting on the project has been designed to minimize energy uses with the type of high efficiency fixtures and bulbs that Studio 804 uses in every project. In this case the lighting was also turned into an art installation. The lounge ceiling supports a steel plate fixture that has been perforated with hundreds of small holes, through each a single flexible fiber optic strand passes like an individual hair. At night, the light of each "hair" reflects off the glass louvres and creates a milky way like backdrop for Galileo's Garden.*

POTABLE WATER USAGE

A portion of the plumbing system uses non-potable water to reduce the consumption of domestic drinking water. The rainwater that is not absorbed by the sedum filled roof trays is directed to a cistern. The rainwater is then pumped to the rainset located inside the building. The rainset filters the water from the cistern through a sediment filter as well as a UV light. In addition to filtering the water, the rainset meters the amount of water being used from the cistern. When the cistern runs out of water domestic water serves as a backup to the system. The harvested water is then used to flush toilets and irrigate the interior living walls. The three living walls in the classrooms and lounge are fed through a pressure reduced valve that distributes the appropriate amount to each living wall. The building cuts domestic water usage up to 50 percent.

GALILEO'S PAVILION, 2012

GALILEO'S PAVILION, 2012

ECOHAWKS, THE HILL ENGINEERING AND DEVELOPMENT CENTER, 2013

University of Kansas Campus, Lawrence, Kansas
LEED Platinum Certified

STUDIO 804 AND ECOHAWKS

Much of the developed world's energy resources go to transportation and buildings. Studio 804 and the EcoHawks are educational programs studying ways to reduce this unsustainable situation and both are graduating students that will take part in the ongoing technological evolution and the shared world economy. It is a natural partnership that the Dean John Gaunt hoped to nurture during the summer of 2012.

He was engaged in conversations with the engineering school and the University architect about Studio 804 taking part in the dramatic expansion of the engineering school that was happening across the University of Kansas campus. In 2012 The EcoHawks were operating out of an inadequate garage that limited their potential. A new EcoHawk's facility was planned as a small part of the 25,000 square feet Structural Testing and Student Projects Facility that was being built on the University of Kansas west campus. Upon John's urging it was determined that the EcoHawks were worthy of their own building to openly advertise their efforts and that working with Studio 804 was the best way to achieve this.

F *The final kit of parts that make up the rainscreen consists of ½" tubing that runs horizontally and gathers the vertical strips of 1 ½", 3", 6" and 9" aluminum strips that were available on the secondary market after the collapse of the aircraft industry in Wichita, Kansas. The weave is held off the moisture barrier by neoprene shims that support the horizontal tubing but are hidden by the weave. The air space allows the assembly to breathe and any water that does get behind the weave drains to a simple polyethylene plastic vent where it is released. The aluminum horizontals were hand welded to create continuous corners and avoid any trim details that would break the rhythm of the weave.*

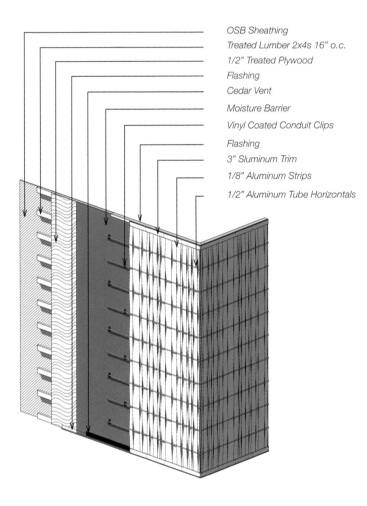

OSB Sheathing

Treated Lumber 2x4s 16" o.c.

1/2" Treated Plywood

Flashing

Cedar Vent

Moisture Barrier

Vinyl Coated Conduit Clips

Flashing

3" Sluminum Trim

1/8" Aluminum Strips

1/2" Aluminum Tube Horizontals

THREE-BAY DESIGN

In August before the students had arrived Rockhill and Associates had quickly devised the overall three-bay form and plan layout which got the project started. It changed very little over the course of the project, it was a simple design that was driven by function and did not try to do more than necessary. I again had to convince students to think about design differently and promised them they would feel full ownership of the building's architecture once they discovered the design challenges that still lie ahead. This proved be dramatically true on this project

as the most defining feature of the building was completely the result of student research and development and likely never would have occurred if we would have deviated from the simple functional forms.

THE WEAVE

The building was going to have large uninterrupted walls of cladding and it was important that these surfaces be turned into a positive feature. A trio of students had studied the technical requirements and precedents for cladding systems and along with the entire group the idea of a woven rainscreen began to emerge. They felt that both the technical aspects of the weave and the use of salvaged aluminum were fitting symbols for the EcoHawks program and I agreed. These three students ended up working on the weave from these first conversations, through mock-ups and to the actual installation of the layered pieces that composed the final design.

The weave went through half a dozen iterations to create a full-scale mock-up that determined the proper scale and hierarchy of the materials. Then at least a half dozen more iterations to determine the materials and connections that would not only be attractive but functional and maintenance free. We were creating a moderately open rainscreen which required a durable drainage plane that would not only prevent moisture from entering the building but would not break down under the daily exposure to the UV rays of the sun. The decision to have the vertical strips of the weave be prominent enhanced this problem. When the strips are running horizontally they act as louvres and shade the moisture barrier. When the strips are run vertically they allow sun to hit portions of the wall at some point on every sunny day of the year. Fortunately, with the increasing of rainscreens there have been advancements in the design of the moisture barriers. We were able to find a membrane that could withstand exposure to the direct sun without UV degradation. This allowed us to install the weave as we desired.

The students researched the aluminum alloys and all the fasteners to make sure the cladding would weather evenly and avoid galvanic action that could lead to unsightly staining or failure. They worked with a representative from the Aluminum Association to confirm their findings and to get suggestions for solutions to the problems they faced. Two of the most important factors were that raw aluminum had to be separated from galvanized metal and that different alloys of aluminum have the potential to create unsightly white rust when in constant contact. Since we were sourcing the aluminum from salvage yards it was hard to expect that it all be the same alloy. We ended up having the horizontal tubing clear anodized to create a separation between them and the vertical strands they support. The rest of the problems were solved with neoprene spacers, butyl tape, and coated fasteners. This process would have been easier if the budget had supported the purchase of thousands of stainless steel fasteners and clips, but it did not. We had to find other, more affordable but dependable fastener options. For example, after many failed attempts during the mock-ups we found that plastic coated, two-hole conduit straps were the perfect way to fasten the horizontal aluminum tubing to the building through neoprene spacers.

ECOHAWKS, THE HILL ENGINEERING AND DEVELOPMENT CENTER, 2013

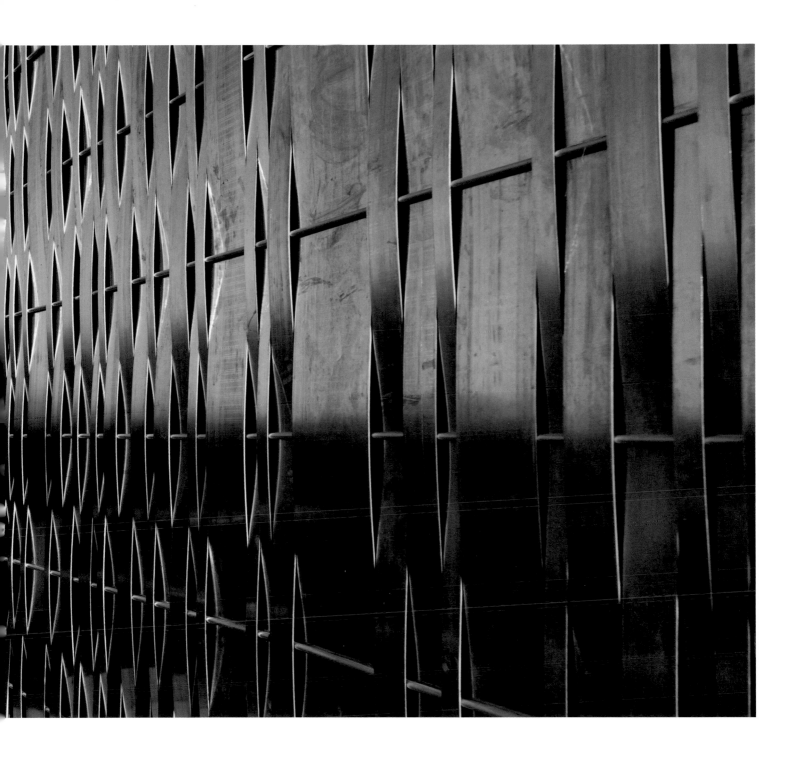

G H

G *The weave creates the effect of a lenticular printed surface as it seems to subtlety change as a person moves. It also changes dramatically with the lighting. During different times of the year or during different weather conditions the siding creates a distinctly different building and it is the characteristic of the building that most visitors are most likely to remember.*

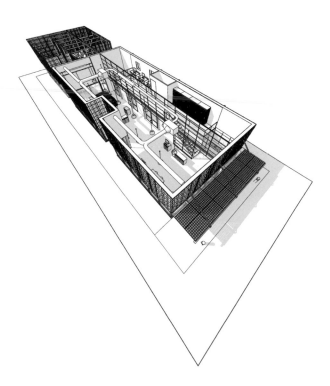

THE DESIGN

The building is divided into three bays. The first two bays support high-bay fabrication work are open to each other and are held to the south side of the building. One of the bays has a car lift mounted to the slab. The work areas are fully daylighted and the concrete slab acts as thermal mass to absorb the sun's heat during the winter. The north side of these bays is stacked with the bathrooms, storage areas and locker rooms as well as the computer research labs that support the hands-on work being done in the shop. The shop and the computer rooms are separated but visually linked by a glass wall that was designed to use salvaged glass panels we still had in stock from previous classes salvage efforts. The computer room flooring is made with post-consumer recycled tires.

The third pod is a detached, open-air mechanical research space. When the design began EcoHawks requested an outdoor work area but I was concerned about the potential for clutter and did not want to add a fenced yard. Also, there was limited space on the site for this work area. After learning what type of work was to be done we designed a multiple story outdoor work area that would be contained in a volume the same size as the other two bays. It is also clad with the weave but is open to the air at the ground level and has no roof. The weave acts as a wind and vision screen supported by a steel frame and backed with cement fiber board. The steel frame also supports a stair and the outdoor work decks which were made with 12,000 lbs. of steel grating found in a salvage yard that we had galvanized. From the upper deck, there is access to the roof of the first two bays which is covered with a photovoltaic array that powers the building.

I   *We were not asked to install the typically functioning garage door as would likely have been required if it were being used multiple times a day. Instead, vehicles are only occasionally brought in through an aluminum framed glass sliding and folding door that is incorporated into the storefront system at the front elevation.*

Extending above this garage door as well as the adjacent entry door is a large awning with a structural steel frame that supports sheets of glass with built-in photovoltaics. The awning advertises upon approach the type of work being done inside the building. The EcoHawks not only wanted this facility to house their work but they also wanted it to help promote the program. They asked for the equivalent of a car showroom to educate visitors and gain support for their efforts.

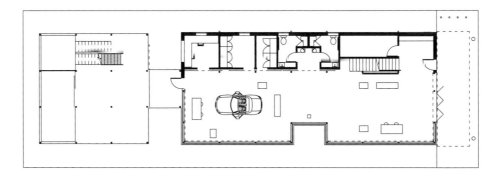

First Floor Plan

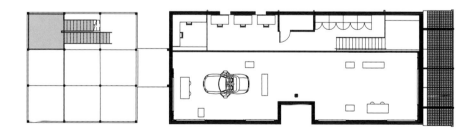

Second Floor Plan

ECOHAWKS, THE HILL ENGINEERING AND DEVELOPMENT CENTER, 2013

J L
―――
K

J L *The work being done in this outdoor bay requires a degree of security, so the ground level is screened with a stainless steel mesh that has a sliding gate where the bays meet. The mesh was purchased from the manufacturer of conveyor belts. We found that we could purchase a high quality, heavy gauge stainless steel screen for significantly less through this source than we could from those selling "architectural" products. We devised our own system for fastening the mesh to the steel frame as well as the concrete slab and could achieve an enclosure that offered security while matching the quality of the rest of the building without crippling our budget.*

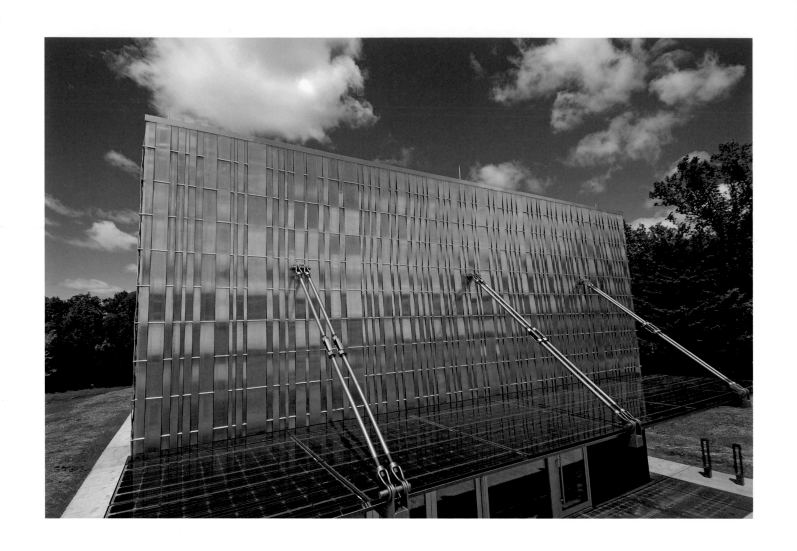

ECOHAWKS, THE HILL ENGINEERING AND DEVELOPMENT CENTER, 2013

AEROGEL PANELS

After years of doing fixed louvres to control the sun I was determined to avoid them on this project. Not only do fixed louvres have limitations but it was important to give the EcoHawks the flexibility to manage the daylight levels and the daily heat gain on their own. The shop work was being done inside the south facing glass walls and if they were not able to manually control the presence of the sun it had the potential to interfere with the work they do.

There was also the concern about heat loss at night. The building was designed to take advantage of heat storage in the mass of the concrete floor, but we were likely to lose much of this heat through the glass unless we spent a large portion of the budget on a high-performance glazing system. In this case the salvaged insulated glass units had already been found at minimal cost and were going to be used in a thermally broken storefront system. We considered many different options to control the sun and add insulation but all of them would limit daylight or create extreme shadows which would be a negative in a mechanical shop where even light is desired for the work.

We decided to explore the use of the translucent and insulating features of aerogel to create movable screens that would address these problems. Aerogel is an ultralight, silica based material with the lowest level of thermal conductivity of any known solid. NASA had for years used it to insulate the space shuttles and is now part of many architectural applications.[1] I had long been interested in using it but had been stopped by the costs as well as the complications of working with a material lighter than air. We reached out to representatives from aerogel suppliers as well as from the aluminum, polycarbonate, glazing and garage door industries to help us create a series of remote operable translucent panels that can be raised and lowered at the push of the button.

To create another level of sun control at the work floor we set operable sun shades between the glass walls and the Aerogel assemblies. These shades can be lowered to reduce glare while still allowing the occupants to see outside.

1) The National Aeronautics and Space Administration NASA website "NASA Spinoff: Technology Transfer Program" Describes examples of NASAs originating technology transferring to consumer goods. The description of aerogel is at: https://spinoff.nasa.gov/Spinoff2010/cg_2.html

M N

M The students of Studio 804 regularly attend the Greenbuild International Conference and Expo. They make connections with representatives in the industry and keep the program abreast of the new developments in sustainable building technology.

N The 40mm polycarbonate panels are filled with aerogel beads to create an R-11 insulated layer that works with the glass wall assembly for a composite performance that would meet the quality of many solid exterior walls while still offering the benefits of 38 percent light transmittance

ECOHAWKS, THE HILL ENGINEERING AND DEVELOPMENT CENTER, 2013

THE HILL ENGINEERING
RESEARCH & DEVELOPMENT CENTER

THE FORUM AT MARVIN HALL, 2014

University of Kansas Campus, Lawrence, Kansas
LEED Platinum Certified

MARVIN HALL

Marvin hall is an Oread limestone structure designed by architect John F. Stanton and opened in 1909 at what was then the west edge of the University of Kansas campus. It is now part of the historic district surrounding Jayhawk Boulevard - the main artery running through the original 19th century campus on top of Mount Oread. It housed the engineering school until 1968 when they moved to a new building and The School of Architecture and Design was created. Architecture students have filled Marvin Hall since. It has gone through several renovations to modernize its infrastructure and make it more aesthetically pleasing but as of 2013 the building still had significant problems. First, the main entry from Jayhawk Boulevard was less than inviting as the foyer died unceremoniously into a nondescript cross corridor. Second, there was not a place for assembly, all architectural lecture classes, visiting speakers and special presentations had to happen elsewhere on campus, often in rooms not very inspiring for the discussion of architecture. And, lastly there had never been a "there" in Marvin Hall - a living room for students and faculty to interact, a place to welcome visitors, an obvious place to meet a friend.

THE FORUM

John Gaunt became the dean of the School of Architecture and Design in 1994 and envisioned The Forum as an addition to Marvin Hall that would address these needs. Given the typical University budget constraints he had little hope of his dream being realized in the traditional way projects are built for the University.

A B

A *Marvin Hall is on Jayhawk Boulevard at the heart of the University of Kansas Campus and the entire district is on the National Register of Historic Places. The Forum was added to the back, south elevation of the building.*

H We had access to mid-20th century tapestries that we saw as perfect for the commons. We wanted this to be a neutral space, not a space filled with exhibits or informational displays selling the University or school. Even when it is functioning as a foyer for the lecture hall we wanted a room that promotes relaxed gathering. From the beginning, it was the living room of Marvin Hall and a living room profits from presence of art. We designed and detailed the commons to frame the tapestries at each end. We kept the material palette of the original Marvin Hall by carefully restoring the original plaster walls and painting them white. The floors are steel plate and the ceiling is the exposed timber frame of Marvin Hall. All the furniture is minimal and restrained in form and color. This composition of space and material creates a quiet backdrop that allows the tapestries to fill the room with color and draw the eye to their soothing presence. Once the jury room was gutted we were left with the original plaster walls as well as the exposed timber floor frame above. We were happy to incorporate these elements into our design.

I The existing jury room was removed to create a commons "living room" as well as a foyer for The Forum that can be used for receptions. It also strengthens the entry to Marvin Hall as an axis now extends from the front doors, through the lobby, to the commons.

the state serving its widespread campus and governmental entities with standard ways to operate. It was no one's fault, but I knew trying to meld their way of operating with Studio 804s one-stop-shop, improvisational ways would be far from seamless.

During every Studio 804 project - and even more so for a project as complicated as The Forum - the students continue to develop the design as the building is under construction. We produce the required construction documents to get a building permit but because of the tight schedule and the fact that we subcontract very little we are continuously working to perfect and complete the design. The students have had almost no experience so I give considerable forethought to these tasks. We meet as a group each morning to discuss that day's work - what needs to be purchased, who needs to be contacted and what problems need to be addressed. For example, for every trade we take on ourselves, be it concrete, framing, roofing, glazing, or the curtain wall installation the students produce shop drawings of adequate specificity to fully integrate the work with the overall architectural design.

To the credit of nearly everyone involved in overseeing The Forum, we were treated respectfully and in the end permitted to work in a manner necessary to get the work done while remaining true to our one-stop-shop ways. It would have been easy for any number of offices or individuals to remain inflexible and insist on standard bidding and procurement. If they had, this project likely would have been impossible. I understand how difficult this was for some and will always be grateful for their cooperation.

Floor Plan:
1) Lecture Hall
2) Jury Room
3) The Commons
4) Hallway
5) Entry from Jayhawk Boulevard

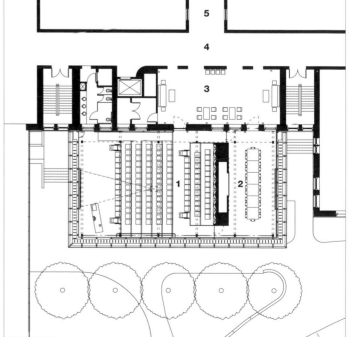

H
—
I

THE DUAL WALL

For a lecture hall to be comfortable for students and speakers alike the conditions need to be predictable and consistent. Passive strategies to save energy typically require a tolerance for temperature swings and varying levels of daylight with the potential for glare.

In 2013 vented dual wall assemblies were relatively new to the architectural world and very new to the US. Due to moisture and overheating concerns they had been limited to specific climates for specific uses but with the new technologies being developed and now available this was changing. I not only saw it as a perfect solution for the glass box of The Forum but as an exceptional learning experience for the students. They would be creating a highly-integrated heating and air conditioning system that would employ several sensors in communication with a weather station on the roof. In addition, they would have to figure out how to coordinate this unique facade with the other allied disciplines such as the structural system, the rest of the mechanical components, the LEED requirements and the acoustic performance of the spaces, to name just a few.

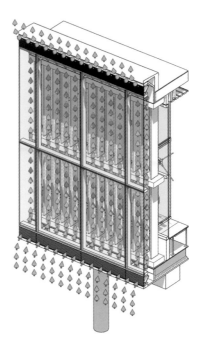

The German company Transsolar is a climate engineering firm that studies the seasonal fluctuations of the sun, wind, heat, light and other energy flows that impact a building. They formulate building solutions based on the local climate, the needs of the user and the goals of the designer. For years, I had been aware the dynamic facades they were helping create for buildings in Europe. With an office in New York they were creating a portfolio of work in the US. They appealed to me as collaborators for Studio 804 because they are respectful of the architect and client and want to work as part of a team to find innovative sustainable design solutions that support the poetic and scientific goals of the project. I felt they would work well with students and would engage them intellectually rather than dictate to them.

Once we had the science behind the concept in place we met regularly with Henderson Engineers who were working on the mechanical systems, the damper manufactures, fan suppliers and our glazing supplier. We worked to find the right balance between the glass coatings and insulation, damper sizes and location, louvre operation, and fan assistance to assure the dual wall assembly would be able to operate at a maximum efficiency during any weather condition without hampering the use of the space with glare, overheating, excess air movement or noise. We also had to assure that there would be no issues with condensation at any of the transition points in the assembly where solar or mechanically heated air meets cool dry air.

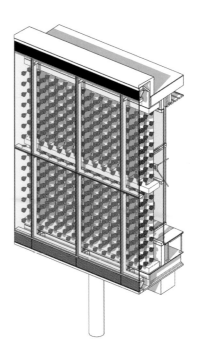

J *Dual Wall Studies: After our conversations with Transsolar we produced studies of the dual wall and how it would operate through the year. To be viable in Lawrence, Kansas we knew it had to operate in the extreme cold and the humid heat and it had to do it without creating condensation that would become trapped in the wall. With Transsolar we proposed a system using sensors and various dampers to adapt the dual wall to the daily conditions.*
1) During hot summer days, it keeps the inner glass wall cool by shading it with the louvres and venting hot air out the top while bringing cooler air in from the shaded underside below.
2) During the cold winter days, the dampers are closed and the dual wall acts as a warm blanket of air surrounding the addition.
3) During nice spring autumn days when fresh air can assist in conditioning the dual pulls outdoor air into the space and distributes it through the floor where it enters the hall through openings at the tiers.

THE FORUM AT MARVIN HALL, 2014

P Q

Q *The automated louvres follow the path of the sun and are in communication with a weather station on the roof of the building so the sun's penetration into the space can efficiently be managed at any time. They allow the daylight to reduce the need of artificial lighting while also controlling glare. They also control the amount of direct sunlight in contact with the interior layer of the dual wall that creates the perimeter enclosure of the conditioned space.*

THE MECHANICAL SYSTEM

The dual wall can be vented in several ways with thermally insulated automated dampers. If sensor readings show that conditions are right for fresh air to assist, or take over for cooling, the primary mechanical systems will adapt or shut down. The dual wall will then operate to promote the cross-ventilation needed. The warm air in the dual wall will be released through open dampers at the parapet of the outer layer of the west dual wall which will then pull air through open dampers behind the ceiling over the speaker at the top of the interior layer of the west dual wall. This displaced air will pull fresh air through open dampers at the bottom of outer layer of the east dual wall and into the floor plenum. From there it will seep into the lecture hall at a low velocity through openings at all the stair risers. If the natural conditions will not create the needed air displacement acoustically insulated fans in the floor plenum will automatically be engaged and will assist. During the hot summer months, the louvres are programmed to constantly shade the interior glass wall of the dual wall. Dampers located on the outer layer on all three dual wall elevations will open at both the top and bottom to allow the rising hot air to escape while bringing fresh cooler air in from the bottom. The dampers between the dual wall and the floor plenum will remain closed and the space will be mechanically cooled. During cold winter days, all the dampers will be closed, and the dual wall will trap the sun's heat to create a "warm blanket" that surrounds and insulates the addition. If the events inside permit the louvres can also be set to allow the sun to penetrate the space and passively warm The Forum.

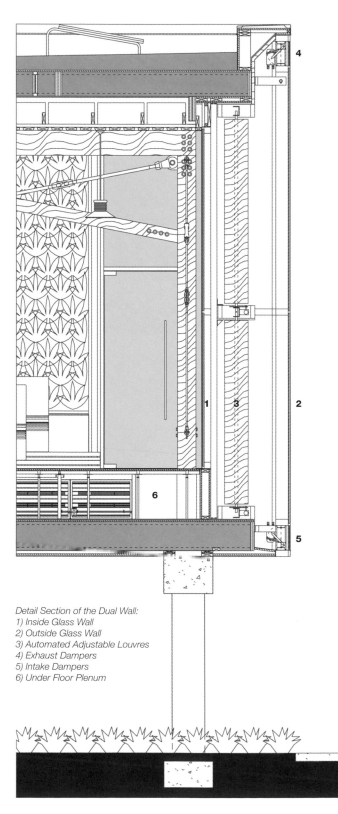

Detail Section of the Dual Wall:
1) Inside Glass Wall
2) Outside Glass Wall
3) Automated Adjustable Louvres
4) Exhaust Dampers
5) Intake Dampers
6) Under Floor Plenum

THE FORUM AT MARVIN HALL, 2014

THE GLULAM FRAME

A douglas fir glulam timber frame supports the roof of The Forum. We designed six evenly spaced timber bents and worked with a timber frame manufacturer to prefabricate them and deliver them to the site. The design features timber columns at each end gathered with a flat top chord and a king post with steel tie rods composing a structural truss. After we assembled the components for the timber bents we lifted them into place as complete units with a crane. The legs pass through the floor frame and are set in galvanized steel boots that we anchored to the concrete beams that support the floor frame. Steel tie rod diagonals run perpendicular to the timber bents to create a rigid frame to support the roof loads.

Since we insisted on the shape and size of the timber bents and would not allow them to be altered to be more typical in their structural dynamics the manufacturer and structural engineer would not sign off on the structural drawings for lateral loads unless the structure was reinforced. Our design was adequate for the dead load requirements and we felt that Marvin Hall would offer plenty of lateral support but rather than dispute this finding we decided to make the most of the situation. We designed, fabricated and installed steel X-brace frames that act as lateral reinforcing at each end of The Forum. Both are significant architectural features in their space - the one in the lecture hall supports the projection screen. Gracefully solving this problem during the construction process to end up with a solution that improved the finished building directly supports the ideas behind an experiential learning laboratory such as Studio 804.

09

ZERO ENERGY HOUSES

After completing The Forum, Studio 804 turned back to addressing housing concerns. I felt the educational opportunities offered by building a house were equal to, or possibly even greater, than the larger buildings we had been doing for a few years. The students are not advanced enough in their understanding of building to fully profit from all the complications the commercial buildings add to a year for Studio 804.

They can easily be swept up in the momentum of the project and begin to lean too hard on the consultants and sub-contractors who are required by code and necessity to play a larger role. Soon, the students are managing who will solve the problems rather than hands-on solving them themselves. It is still a valuable experience that prepares them for the profession but is not the same experience that had shaped Studio 804. Since building The Forum we have focused on houses targeted for net zero energy use in established neighborhoods in Lawrence.

1301 NEW YORK STREET HOUSE, 2015

East Lawrence Neighborhood, Lawrence, Kansas
LEED Platinum Certified
Passive House Institute US (PHIUS) Certified

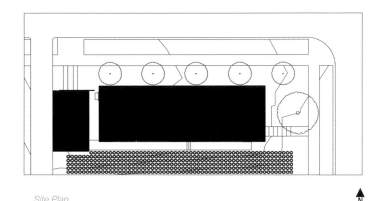

Site Plan

N

FINDING A PROJECT

After helping the 2014 class finish The Forum it became time for the 2015 class to work on their own project. While The Forum was being finished Rockhill and Associates spent some time trying to formulate a public project in Eudora, Kansas that would transition to Studio 804 when they were ready. The funding and coordination proved to be too difficult for the short time frame and I was having doubts about another commercial project.

Although the run of educational buildings had been architecturally fulfilling and I do not regret the effort. I had begun to question whether these complex projects were any greater an educational opportunity than a high-performance house. Not only does the complexity of the buildings require me to guide the design with a stronger hand, but unlike houses, the commercial projects require Rockhill and Associates to be the architects of record and a much stronger presence from the various engineers is required.

Working on a house is simple by comparison but still offers the chance for the type of comprehensive problem solving that will be required of future architects. Houses still have a sewer tap and utilities, they still need mechanical, electrical and plumbing systems and for the type of sustainable projects we will be doing the students will still be working with innovative technologies that will require them to do research and reach out to experts. At this point in their development it is important for them to learn about property setbacks and easements and how to layout a foundation and submit for a building permit. It is important for them to learn to confidently negotiate with local historic commissions and neighborhood associations. It is beneficial to thoroughly design, detail and build a kitchen or bathroom, both of which require them to think functionally, aesthetically

and technically. In doing this they will learn lessons that transfer to the larger more complex problems while working at a scale more compatible with their current skills and knowledge.

PROPERTY

We searched Lawrence for a piece of property that would support the type of house we were interested in building. Studio 804 ended up purchasing a north facing corner lot in the East Lawrence Neighborhood. The market for property near downtown Lawrence is very strong and even in lesser neighborhoods vacant lots are rare and expensive. This site had once been a gas station and the old tanks were still in the ground and would need to be removed. This triggers a string of EPA requirements for developing and selling the property that intimidated other potential buyers. I had worked on the removal of buried tanks with Rockhill and Associates and had experience with the process. It also fit Studio 804s mission to develop a brownfield site.

A
——
B C D

B C *The restrictions inherent in the site had a significant hand in the final design. It is a narrow corner site that faces north. By the time we removed the setbacks and held the building off the south property line - to promote passive solar gain and some sunny outdoor spaces - we had little room left to place a building of the size we felt necessary for the market we were targeting.*

D *Not only is it unlikely we would get a building loan if we tried but is also difficult or impossible for potential buyers to get a traditional mortgage loan for one of our projects. There are few comparables for the high-performance houses we are building, let alone one set amongst houses of significantly lesser value. The banks do not like to loan on a building seen as exceeding the neighborhood. For this reason, when designing this house, we targeted buyers who could pay for the house with cash and avoid these mortgage pitfalls that had caused us problems in the past.*

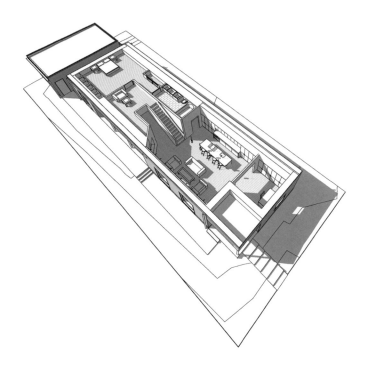

As with the Springfield House we had built in 2009 - before we started building commercial buildings - we bought the property, paid for the materials and built the house ourselves. We did not have to involve outside investors, banks or community development groups who would then expect to have a say about the design and the target market.

INFILL PROJECTS

This project is another example of modern, sustainable housing in an established neighborhood of inconsistent quality where the positives outweigh the negatives. It is within walking distance of a grocery store, grade school, a community center and the cultural vibrancy of downtown Lawrence. It is a three-bedroom, two and a half bathroom 2,000 square-foot house that is LEED Platinum and PHIUS certified. It is also targeted for net zero energy use. It features an air tight, highly insulated thermal envelope, efficient light fixtures and appliances as well as a high performance mechanical system that incorporates an energy recovery ventilator as well as mini splits.

In healthy communities such as Lawrence there has been a trend toward empty nesters and retirees moving from the suburbs back to the urban amenities and proximities the suburbs do not offer. Some residents in the East Lawrence Neighborhood saw this as an example of gentrification and were against the project feeling that new development should focus on affordability. I am sensitive to this criticism but feel it more apt if the house was simply focused on location, luxury and size. Our design is focused on the future of sustainability in housing.

THE DESIGN

The house is an unassuming gable form that runs the length of the narrow corner lot and opens away from the traffic of 13th street while promoting passive solar gain and daylighting through large high-performance German manufactured triple pane windows along its south elevation. The standing seam roof, the half round gutters and the minimal trim detailing at the openings are all done to emphasize the visually rich texture of the siding and to maximize the impact of the universal building form and its minimal composition.

The plan consists of a large, open living area that is anchored by a sleek kitchen designed for serious cooking as well as entertainment. The ceiling extends all the way to the peak of the gable and the 18" deep walls open to a bio-swale that runs the length of the south side of the house to capture storm water and supports a variety of native plants. The rest of the house is composed of smaller bedrooms and flexible use spaces as well as the upstairs master bedroom suite that includes a balcony-like office with a view into the living area. With the walls being so thick we were not required to add exterior louvres to control the sun, the walls themselves work as adequate shade during the summer days and the unencumbered windows work better for winter solar gain.

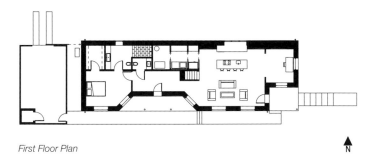

First Floor Plan

N

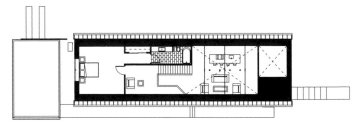

Second Floor Plan

E
—
F

E F *Designing and building a functioning kitchen offers the students many of the types of challenges they will face in larger commercial projects but at a scale that is more manageable at this point in their education and within a single school year.*

1301 NEW YORK STREET HOUSE, 2015

1200 PENNSYLVANIA STREET HOUSE, 2016

East Lawrence Neighborhood, Lawrence, Kansas
LEED Platinum Certified

ANOTHER HIGH-PERFORMANCE HOUSE

Building Studio 804's first house in a few years with the class of 2015 confirmed my suspicion that students would learn as much or more working on a high-performance house as they would learn if I continued to pursue the more logistically complicated commercial buildings. This did not mean I was going to tolerate any sort of architectural retreat. We were going to continue to pursue innovation in material use, energy consumption and we were still going to create buildings with a high intrinsic design value. Just as the students who had worked on the university buildings had to manage the sun, keep water out and find resourceful ways to combine an air tight building envelope with a highly efficient mechanical system so would these students. They just wouldn't seek state approval for a code footprint or debate occupancy requirements with the fire marshal. The class of 2016 would have their own less time consuming challenges. I did not plan to demand less of them but I did like the thought of having a building permit early enough to have a foundation in place before the first freeze.

The 1600 square-foot house at 1200 Pennsylvania has two-bedrooms, two-bathrooms and is designed to be fully accessible. It achieved LEED Platinum certification while also living up to the Passive House Institute US (PHIUS) standards while not incurring the added expensive of certification. It is in the same historic neighborhood as 1301 New York Street and like that house was designed to appeal to the empty nesters and retirees who are moving from the suburbs into established older surroundings. It features an air tight, highly insulated thermal envelope, energy star rated light fixtures and appliances as well as a high performance mechanical system. These design characteristics in combination with a photovoltaic array on the roof and the building's proper orientation to take advantage of the sun for heat and the breezes and shade for cooling - again assuring the house will require little or no expenditures for energy over a calendar year.

ENGAGING THE SITE

The house occupies a lot and a half making up the southeast corner of a quiet intersection in the East Lawrence neighborhood. The extra space offered the opportunity to generously engage the site. For reasons of time, the use of prefabrication, or simply because we felt it was the appropriate design solution the Studio 804 houses had typically been objects on their

A *Two gables that make up the front of the house are brought together by the entry foyer that acts as the hinge that gathers the entire house and site. The resulting front elevation is unique while still being respectful of its neighbors.*

sites. For this house, on this site, I hoped to use the building to create strong outdoor spaces that would define the house as much as the interior. We arranged three gable forms to create a south facing courtyard that is the focal point of the house, as nearly every room opens to it through full height windows.

THE INTERIOR
The north gable holds the living room and the two-bedrooms. It opens through a band of south facing windows to the courtyard. The eastern gable is adjacent to the alley and holds the one car garage and storage. Between it and the north gable is a concrete tornado shelter. The western gable is connected to the north gable by an entry foyer and houses a large kitchen and dining area. It is the social heart of the residence and has views to the rest of the house, the courtyard and the street.

To keep the interior streamlined and to allow the rooms to feel larger than they are, all the doors are custom made surface sliders. The windows are high performance triple pane units that assure air tightness. They have been located to promote solar heat gain, minimize heat loss and promote cross ventilation. In the living room a low band of operable windows line the south wall while a high band line the north wall. The floors are all concrete slabs coated with semi -gloss grey epoxy. All the cabinets are off the shelf boxes with custom doors we made in the shop.

There was some backlash in the neighborhood about another "expensive" house being built in the neighborhood. People covet the properties close to downtown and the property values have responded. As we learned the year before at 1301 New York Street there is understandable concern about gentrification and the lack of affordable housing. I take these issues seriously and we have addressed affordable housing over the years but at this time, in Lawrence, I prefer to continue to lead by example in sustainable design while trying to keep costs as low as possible and design at a scale that shows respect for the surroundings. If there is to be a day when net zero energy use housing is ubiquitous it will require the openness to experimentation and the willingness to absorb risk that Studio 804 can offer. The products and techniques we are using need to be used so the profession can learn by experience. Just as ten years ago LED lights were expensive, limited in options and uncommon, energy recovery ventilators, photovoltaic systems, advanced rainscreens, air tight construction techniques and energy efficient fixtures are becoming more common and affordable today. This process must continue. It is part of Studio 804's mission to educate graduates who are ready to jump in and take part in the positive directions the profession is heading.

B *The courtyard opens to the sun but is protected from the north winds maximizing its use throughout the year. We composed the combination of concrete slab, pavers, gravel and a retaining wall to finish the outdoor room. It also includes a rain garden that collects the storm runoff to support the growth of native plants and to allow the water to absorb into the subsurface of the site.*

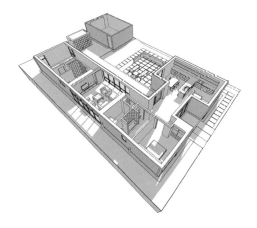

Floor Plan

THE ENVIRONS

The property is in the environs of a state registered historic property. Before we could get a building permit the students had to submit the design for review to the Lawrence Historic Resources Administrator and then eventually on to the entire Commission. They then decide during one of their monthly public hearings whether to approve the work or not. The approach here - as it has been on all the projects I have worked on that involve historic properties since Studio 804s first project, The Barber School - is to respect the forms and character of the surrounding buildings while creating something distinctly new. Most people in the state and national historic review offices feel this is the more prudent path than resorting to overt historic mimicry. At a local level, you never know what might be decided. Our proposal blended with the context by arranging common and unassuming gable forms and then finishing them with historically available materials such as wood siding, standing seam roofs, and half round gutters. It was made distinct by keeping the gables elemental, with no cross gables or dormers and by using minimal trim detailing. We wanted the most immediate feature to be the timeless beauty of the of the horizontally run cedar.

This was a valuable experience for the students as they had to defend the design. There were those commission members who wanted to debate the number of windows, their placement on the elevations and the lack of a front porch. It is not good enough to simply use sustainability as an excuse for limiting windows on the north elevation or saying we have a large courtyard as a reason for not including a front porch. We had to research other buildings in the environs and present historical precedence for what we were proposing. Despite what we saw as an obviously respectful solution the public meeting was a hair-raising experience and we were not sure until the last minute if we were going to be approved.

When devising this strategy, we knew the choice of siding would be vital to the success of the project. We were fortunate to find an internet lead to Ancestral Wood Products, a company that specializes in distributing reclaimed wood. They had access to a trove of reclaimed western red cedar available when the US Forest Service decided to dismantle several railroad bridge trestles that had been built in the early days of logging and had become dangerous or problematic. This old growth lumber was of unparalleled quality that we would not be able to responsibly purchase today. The logs were rough sawn to approximately 3 x 6 size before being shipped. It was a wonderful design opportunity as the students took this raw material into our warehouse and shaped and surfaced it until it was part of a highly refined rainscreen.

C E F G H *Studio 804 is increasingly using sustainably harvested and salvaged wood for both the structure and finishes which promotes carbon sequestration.*

C D
—————
E F G H

I J
—
K

J *All the floors are concrete slabs placed by the students and used as a solar mass for passive heating.*

K *The entire building envelope, including the concrete floor, is insulated.*

1330 BROOK STREET HOUSE, 2017

Brook Creek Neighborhood, Lawrence, Kansas
LEED Platinum Certified

BUILDING IN A FEMA FLOOD PLAIN

As seems to be the case nearly every summer, I was running out of time to determine on what and where the next class would do their work. With the success of the houses we had done since we built The Forum I wanted to continue in this direction. I had considered doing a smaller affordable project on one of the small lots on the fringes of the old housing stock on the eastern side of Lawrence, but the students join Studio 804 anxious to work with the type of technology we have been exploring for the last decade. These technologies and techniques are important to the future of architecture as well as preparing them for their professional careers.

One of the locations I had been considering with Rockhill and Associates for a small house was two adjacent sites in the FEMA flood zone that the owner had built up with compacted earth to create a buildable site above the flood plain. They were easily the ugliest building sites I had ever considered tackling. They were a weed covered mound of dirt surrounded by housing that was not going to help attract a buyer.

What would help attract a buyer is that the property was within a couple of blocks of a recreation center and across the street from a very attractive park with a stream, nice green spaces, large mature trees and a nicely equipped playground. It is also with a couple of blocks from an elementary school. If this neighborhood followed the rest of Lawrence and began to be revitalized this park would be an anchor to the neighborhood and this house would be at the heart of it.

The lots had been for sale for a long time and were going to be much less expensive than the typical Lawrence vacant property - even in this relatively tattered part of town. I decided Studio 804 could embrace the misfit character of the site and turn it into a positive. The money we would save on the property could be put toward the quality of the house. I also liked the idea that I would have a building site in my pocket for the next year's class if it was needed.

A final factor was that these lots, like most of the neighborhood, are 40' wide x 132' deep. This makes for a narrow footprint for building, meaning we would have to build a smaller house than the last two. This was fine since my 2017 class only had 10 students. If we were going to build to the standards of the previous classes, we would have to keep the house smaller and simpler than the last two.

LUSTRON HOUSES

Design inspiration can come from unexpected places. During the summer of 2016 I was approach by the sales representative for a metal panel system. He was a former student from the pre-Studio 804 days who had followed the program and thought he had some panels we would be interested in. Rock Chalk Park, a large sports park, was being built on the western edge of Lawrence and the Jayhawk Tennis Center was to be sided with their enamel-coated, insulated steel panels. A significant number of panels had suffered surface paint damage before installation. The manufacturer was willing to give them to us if we could use them and came and got them. Typically used for warehouse applications, the insulated metal panels are comprised of three inches of high performance rigid insulation sandwiched between layers of steel. The panels snap together via a sophisticated tongue-and-groove joint, and they provide an R-value of 25. All we would have to do is sand the damage and repaint the exterior surfaces and we would have a quality siding material for almost no costs. At first, I was not all attracted to the aesthetics of these panels considering the uninspired way they are typically used. But, I reminded myself, there are no bad materials – just bad uses. While building the net zero energy use houses we have had to add layers of rigid board insulation outside the framed building envelope. We have used sheathed systems like Hunter Panels or add sheathing over layers of rigid board insulation ourselves. This is labor intensive and costly. If we used these panels we could achieve the needed insulation and have a finished low maintenance siding in one step. I just had to re-think how they could be detailed and what sort of building form they would enhance.

I have always admired the Lustron homes of the 1950's. Their metal panel siding, low slung mid-20th century modernism and clean detailing were a good architectural result to come from the optimistic faith in the future in America after World War II and the pressing need for housing for returning GI's. Using these insulated metal panels, we chose to create an homage to these houses.

After doing a couple of gabled houses in the historic environs of the East Lawrence Neighborhood I was ready to work with a different roof form and this site gave us the freedom to do so. Since the house was going to be small and we had access to a stock of engineered lumber I thought we could do a simple rectangular box with a flat roof. Like the Lustron house, we would bring architectural significance to the simple form with quality materials and detailing.

A B C

B C *Lustron house were built in the 1950's to help with the post war demand for housing in America. Unlike some of the unfortunate developments that occurred at this time such as asbestos siding or Levittown the Lustron houses have proven to be timeless with their simple forms, steel detailing and metal panel siding.*

D E

D *The ground cover and site plantings are drought-resistant native species. A large native cottonwood tree at the northeast corner of the lot was preserved.*

E *When I first saw the site, it was an ugly mound of weed covered dirt that created a building site above the FEMA flood plain. When the house was completed this rise in elevation adds to the presence of the house and improves the view to the Brook Creek Park across the street.*

Site Plan

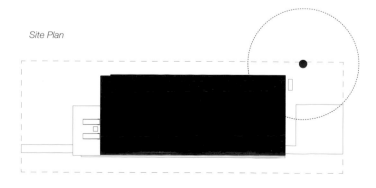

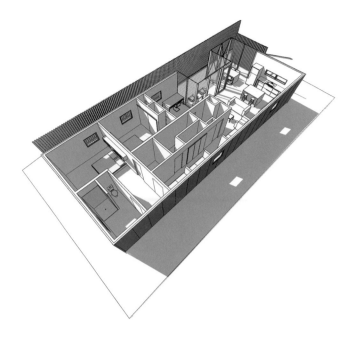

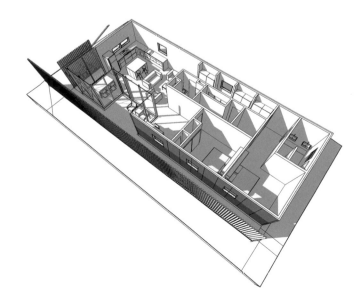

F G

F *The house is a simple rectangle with a flat roof. The roof plane extends to steel lattice structures creating covered walkways that connect the sunny uncovered patio at the front of the house to the covered semi-private patio in "the notch" at the entry.*

Floor Plan

front patio	master bedroom
entry notch	master bathroom
dining room	hall with storage
kitchen	bathroom
living room	laundry
flex room	mechanical room
bedroom	walk in closet

THE DESIGN

We chose to build on the southernmost of the two sites. If I did build on the adjacent site with the next year's class I did not want to be pinned between two close houses. With the narrow lots, this meant the house would be close to its neighbor to the south. We did not want to turn our back on the southern exposure, so we explored ways to screen our house from the neighbor while still allowing the sunlight to enter the house. Studio 804 has had a long running relationship with a steel supplier who always encourages us to use steel tube. With the Lustron houses in mind, we explored the possibility of creating a steel "lattice" with vertically run, closely spaced, steel tubes that would extend along the south edge of the site for the depth of the house. As the design developed we did the same thing for the west, front elevation to mitigate the western sun and screen the view into the house from the street.

I knew the house was going to be a simple rectangle in plan. After that, we had to figure out the smallest layout possible that would meet our architectural aspirations while still achieving a three-bedroom appraisal. Building in this location, I was not as

confident we would find a buyer who could purchase the house without a significant mortgage as had happened the previous two years. I wanted it to appraise for as much as possible to aid that process since there are no comparables close buy. Many of the properties within the nearby blocks would be more valuable if the houses did not exist and lots were vacant.

We were able to get the house down to a flexible 1300 square foot one-story layout. It allows the owner to customize the spaces to fit their personal preferences while also making the house appealing to a wide range of potential buyers. The rectangular plan is broken only by "the notch" along the south elevation. It creates a semi private patio that is visible to the house through floor to ceiling glass walls on all three sides. It is screened from the neighboring house and the street by the steel lattice. From this patio one enters the living room and kitchen that line the north wall. To each side of the notch are flexible, open, light filled spaces. They can be reconfigured to accommodate different functions. The room to the east can easily be used as a third bedroom, an office, an exercise room or as an extension of the living room. The glass-enclosed space at the southwest corner of the house can be used as a dining room, solarium, or reading room. From the living/kitchen area a hallway extends along the north wall of the house which is lined with storage cabinets interrupted by operable windows that support cross ventilation. To the south of the hallway is the bathroom, mechanical room and the second bedroom. The hallway ends at the master bedroom suite at the back of the house.

H   I
___
J

J   *The hanging pendant located in the dining room is an original Louis Poulsen fixture crafted in Denmark and purchased for reuse in this project.*

K L

K L *The cedar soffit was left over from a previous Studio 804 project. Penofin oil provides a natural finish and protects the cedar from weathering.*

MATERIALS

We selected materials based on a desire for longevity and ease of maintenance, including the re-purposed metal panel cladding system and insulated glass units for the southwest glazing. The countertops are cold-rolled steel treated with anti-corrosive and eco-friendly coating. The off the shelf cabinetry is customized with Forest Stewardship Council-certified red oak door fronts with a natural beeswax finish. The floors are poor man's version of terrazzo. Working with students who have never poured concrete - let alone a slab - I cannot expect a perfect finish acceptable for an exposed concrete floor. We had to rent a grinder and use diamond tipped abrasive pads to create a smooth floor. This exposes the aggregate and creates a beautiful, rich floor without the need for finishes that cost money and have the potential to include VOC's that cannot be used inside a house being built to these environmental standards.

We have done flat roofs before and we use white TPO roofing which does not promote the heat island effect and achieves LEED credit. One of the problems for us has been the fact that we reach the point of roofing our projects in the middle of winter. To properly apply the TPO at least three days of 40-degree weather are needed. This does not often happen in middle of winter in Kansas. While developing the roof details we were encouraged to use a new technology for applying the membrane roof that uses induction heat technology to fasten the membrane during any temperature.

RESOURCES

The all-electric house is net-metered with a photovoltaic solar array, consisting of 16 panels with a total output of 4.8 KwH. This will be sufficient to power the house during a typical calendar year with typical power usage. The high-efficiency, low-energy consumption HVAC system uses an energy-recovery ventilator (ERV) to supply fresh air without thermal energy loss. The ERV captures heat released as a byproduct from appliances and the occupants and recirculates it into the system. The open spaces are conditioned by a mini-split unit, while the bedrooms and bathrooms are supplied through a traditional ducted-air system.

Efforts were taken to limit wet wall conditions and consolidate piping. We located the water heater in a central location to reduce piping distances, as well as providing insulated piping to reduce thermal loss. Additionally, we selected fixtures that are WaterSense certified, low-flow fixtures that significantly reduce water usage.

CONCLUSION

When it came time to sell the house I was not interested in basically taking on the same challenge again and building on the adjacent site. I thought I could easily get what I paid out of the second site by packaging it with the house. This would allow the owner a generous space for a large yard, a garden, a garage or carport - or some combination of these. Otherwise the green space was very limited on the narrow lot. Almost all the unbuilt site would be in the setbacks and sloping dramatically from the house down to the street and alley. As had been the case the last two years the house sold easily.

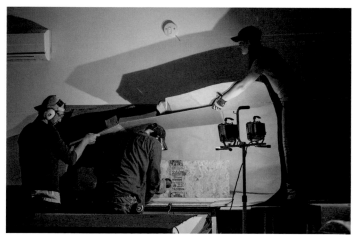

10

THE PAST, PRESENT AND FUTURE

The work of Studio 804 continues, so I continue to look forward as we work on new, innovative, sustainable buildings, but the writing of this book has been a chance to look back. Each year since 1995, a group of mostly young men and women arrive from all over the world to commit themselves to an arduous team effort during which they learn about architecture and themselves.

They have varying backgrounds, each has their own stories, personality and expectations. They all have reasons they have chosen to be in Kansas in August. As a group, these hundreds of energetic, creative, determined students have collectively redefined what a university design/build studio can achieve.

THE PRESENT AND THE FUTURE

1220 E. 12th STREET HOUSE, 2018
Brook Creek Neighborhood, Lawrence, Kansas
LEED Platinum Targeted

THE CURRENT PROJECT

When we took the risk of building a new house in the Brook Creek Neighborhood in 2017 I felt it had the potential to develop quickly along Brook Creek Park. A local design/build/development firm had bought a large property at the north end of the park that was the site of a scrap yard and was in the FEMA flood plain. They cleaned up the property and were selling it as design and build to fit lots for new houses. To help jump start the development they were willing to sell a site to Studio 804.

The eastern most site of this development has a Burr Oak that is the second largest on record in Kansas. The city of Lawrence had intended to buy this property to protect this magnificent tree. Confident this would happen, I asked if we could purchase the adjacent lot. I was already imagining a house that would open to the tree and its site – which feels like an extension of the north end of Brook Creek Park.

All went according to plan until a change in the composition of city commission lead the city to back out of buying the property. This meant it was back on the market and we had already designed and were starting to build a house meant to generously open to this site. My only recourse was to buy the site and protect the tree – and the quality of our current project - myself. I hope to sell the Burr Oak site with the new house. If this proves impossible I will develop the site myself with Studio 804 or Rockhill and Associates in a manner that protects the tree but does not lessen the quality of the Studio 804, 2018 house.

The 1220 E. 12th Street House seeks to maintain the high level of sustainable design we have been working to for years. We intend it to be achieve LEED Platinum certification and approach net zero energy use. As always, we are integrating passive strategies for ventilation and sun shading with photovoltaics and state of the art mechanical, electrical and plumbing systems. It will be Studio 804's first fully integrated smart house. All the blinds, lights, appliance and the heating and air conditioning will be able to communicate with each other and the owner to enhance efficient, responsible and convenient living.

We are applying unobstructed glazing to the East side of the building to fill the house with natural lighting and to open to the Burr Oak tree and Brook Creek Park. The other elevations are finished with fritted glass panels to create a glass box. On the north and west elevations, the glass panels are secured over more of the insulated metal panels we had used during the 2017 project. They provide the insulation we needed but we did not want to use them for the finish siding again. On the south elevation the fritting blocks 80 percent of the sun but let daylight enter the living room at the end of the house.

The 170' X 60' site almost doubles the average lot size of the neighborhood. With this extra space and the right zoning district, we were able to include an accessory dwelling that can be used for rental income or to house an extended family member. It is a fully equipped unit with a kitchen, bedroom, bathroom, and storage. It is located behind the primary house and clad in the same glass and uses the same materials as the primary house.

As we always try to do, we took the potential negative of the site – being in a flood plain – and tried to make it a positive. We carefully composed the building up on the site with compacted earth with the glass boxes of the dwellings perched on concrete plinths off which they cantilever. They seem to float in the park like setting.

WHO DESIGN THE BUILDINGS?

It is done by students! I know some doubt this and point to the fact that I have lately taken a firmer hand in creating initial design concepts as an example to say otherwise. For years, I was reticent to do this for fear of this criticism. I still feel the statement is true even if, starting with the university projects, I have become less patient when steering the overall design. There are always students who start the year wanting Studio 804 to be an extension of their design studio where the vision of the individual is nurtured and foremost to all else. By the time the Mods were being built I still went the through the time-consuming process of schematic design with the students but I knew where I wanted to end up, I was simply subtler about it in those days. No project would ever be the vision of an individual student, just as it is not fully mine by the time it is finished. If, after graduation, the students are lucky enough to be hired by a good design firm they will be working to fulfil the vision of the firm. Within those firms whose work I respect there is always a vocabulary that needs to be nurtured, always a bigger picture within which to place the work and it's never any single persons influence but rather the effort of the collaborative whole. The Studio 804 experience helps to prepare them to be able to express themselves as part of this collective act. As I preach every semester, the overall concept is important, but design development is where special buildings are created. I told the students building the EcoHawks facility that they were working with a simple three pod design, but they designed the aluminum weave cladding that garners everyone's attention. I told 2016's students that they were going to arrange three gables around a south facing courtyard, but they also found, shaped and installed the rainscreen using wood reclaimed from old railroad trestles. These things bind the entire composition together and ultimately define the architecture. The notion that design is a beautiful presentation of a schematic building is what so many classroom studios endorse. I assume this issue will continue to torment me - as it has since the beginning of this venture - unless the approach to teaching architectural design studios changes.

INSTITUTIONAL MEMORY

I am the institutional memory of Studio 804, the one-stop-shop for everything having to do with the work of the program – past, present and future. I like being the lone wolf who is not required to answer to anyone. I sign off on the choice of the project, the site and all design decisions. I see the project through to occupancy and I am the one that starts searching for the next one. Most, if not all, other programs share this load. A staff does the accounting, manages the contracts, supervises the construction, oversees the sale etc. In Studio 804 this is all within my purview but I pass the responsibilities to the students. Therefore, I can call Studio 804 a comprehensive building experience. The students learn to keep records, buy local, pay the bills on time, negotiate with the inspectors, keep consultant costs down, be a good neighbor, and they know what is acceptable when talking to a client or buyer. They learn not to embarrass the rest of the group when they are representing us.

The students do the work but they need to have consistent standards to work toward. Since I am the final voice the construction documents are as good or bad as I let them be, the structural complications are only as difficult as I allow them to be and the final product is as bad or good as I let it be. That said, they are still the last ones on the roof to make sure it does not leak. They are the ones who last adjust a door so it opens and closes properly. No one has ever expected as much from them and I have my doubts that anyone ever will. I'm not easy to work with and I have little patience with their personal hardships. I let them know I believe in them. I have seen many others go through the same struggle they will face only to succeed in ways they could not have imagined and, in the end, to see themselves a stronger, more confident person. I tell them that if they stick with me the end results will prove this.

When I first saw what it meant to students to get out of the classroom and touch the architecture it was exhilarating. I'll never forget when one student, while building our first house turned to me and said, "I had no idea how little I knew," I was hooked.

THE FUTURE

I am pleased with the result of the houses we have done since completing The Forum. I occasionally hear complaints about "just doing houses" as if it were a retreat from the university buildings. I don't know what the future holds, if any interesting larger or unique projects present themselves it is possible I will tackle something new, but anyone who thinks a significant architectural education cannot be attained while building a house is lacking in imagination. In the construction of the houses we have worked with state of the art mechanical systems, we have built butt glazed curtain walls, designed sophisticated rainscreens, installed tapered insulation and new technology in single membrane roofing systems and more. All of this is relevant to architecture at any scale for just about any type of building. In fact, it is the application of those unexpected commercial materials that make the residential work so unique.

So, just as I felt in 2007 when we finished Mod 4 I am happy doing what I am doing right now. But who knows what tomorrow holds. At that time, I did not know what I could do with the students when I had them for an entire school year. I also did not know the housing economy was going to soon collapse. And, I certainly did not know a tornado was going to hit Greensburg, Kansas and that it would lead me and the students to redefine what Studio 804 can be.

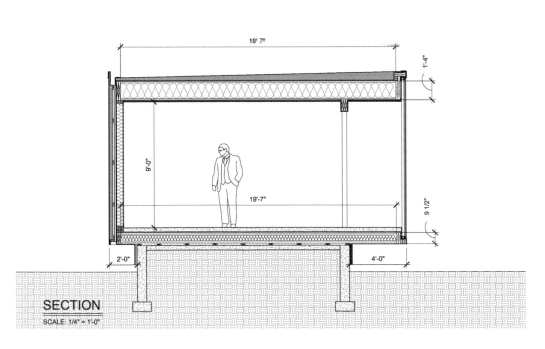

SECTION
SCALE: 1/4" = 1'-0"

10' 7"

1'-4"

9'-0"

19'-7"

9 1/2"

2'-0"

4'-0"

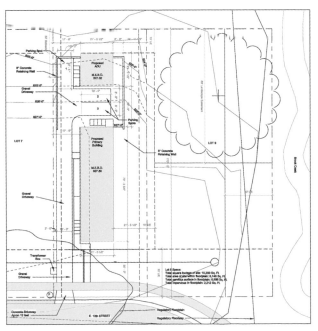

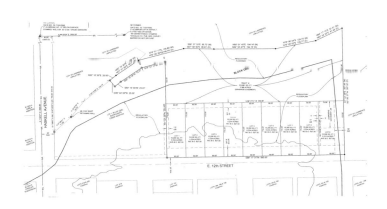

SITE PLAN

THE PRESENT AND THE FUTURE

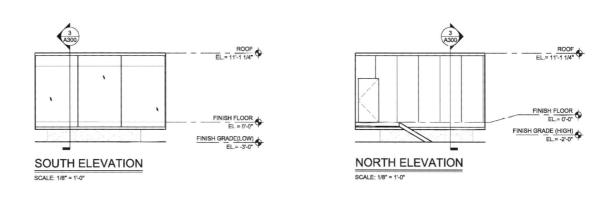

SOUTH ELEVATION
SCALE: 1/8" = 1'-0"

ROOF
EL.= 11'-1 1/4"

FINISH FLOOR
EL = 0'-0"

FINISH GRADE(LOW)
EL.= -3'-0"

NORTH ELEVATION
SCALE: 1/8" = 1'-0"

ROOF
EL.= 11'-1 1/4"

FINISH FLOOR
EL.= 0'-0"

FINISH GRADE (HIGH)
EL.= -2'-0"

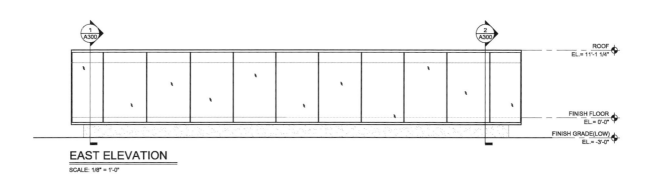

EAST ELEVATION
SCALE: 1/8" = 1'-0"

ROOF
EL.= 11'-1 1/4"

FINISH FLOOR
EL.= 0'-0"

FINISH GRADE(LOW)
EL.= -3'-0"

THE PRESENT AND THE FUTURE

WALL A
SCALE: 1/2" = 1'-0"

METAL SPAN INSULATED PANELS
3" AIR SPACE
VAPOR MEMBRANE
1/2" O.S.B. SHEATHING
5 1/2" STUD FRAME
BREATHABLE MEMBRANE
½" GYP. WALLBOARD

WALL B
SCALE: 1/2" = 1'-0"

1/2" GYP. BD.
5 1/2" STUD FRAME
1/2" O.S.B. SHEATHING
1/2" GYP. BD.

WALL C
SCALE: 1/2" = 1'-0"

1/2" GYP. BD.
5 1/2" STUD FRAME
1/2" GYP. BD.

WALL D
SCALE: 1/2" = 1'-0"

1/2" GYP. BD.
3 1/2" STUD FRAME
1/2" GYP. BD.

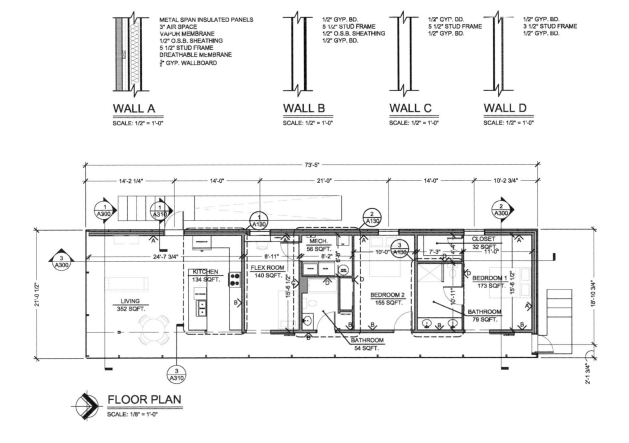

FLOOR PLAN
SCALE: 1/8" = 1'-0"

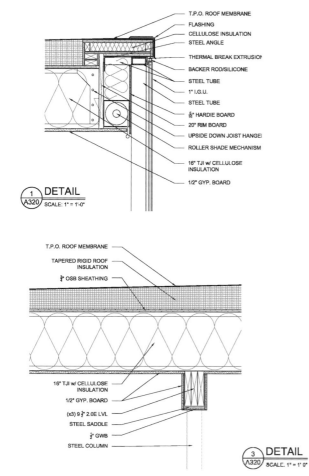

T.P.O. ROOF MEMBRANE
FLASHING
CELLULOSE INSULATION
STEEL ANGLE
THERMAL BREAK EXTRUSION
BACKER ROD/SILICONE
STEEL TUBE
1" I.G.U.
STEEL TUBE
⅝" HARDIE BOARD
20" RIM BOARD
UPSIDE DOWN JOIST HANGER
ROLLER SHADE MECHANISM
16" TJI w/ CELLULOSE INSULATION
1/2" GYP. BOARD

1 DETAIL
A320 SCALE: 1" = 1'-0"

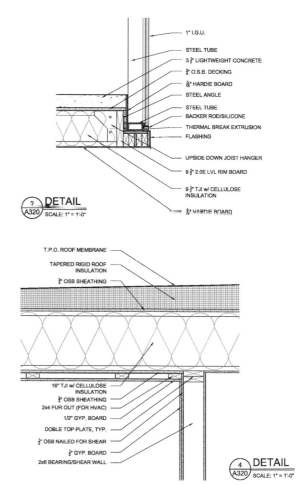

1" I.G.U.
STEEL TUBE
3 ¾" LIGHTWEIGHT CONCRETE
¾" O.S.B. DECKING
⅝" HARDIE BOARD
STEEL ANGLE
STEEL TUBE
BACKER ROD/SILICONE
THERMAL BREAK EXTRUSION
FLASHING
UPSIDE DOWN JOIST HANGER
9 ¾" 2.0E LVL RIM BOARD
9 ¾" TJI w/ CELLULOSE INSULATION
⅝" HARDIE BOARD

? DETAIL
A320 SCALE: 1" = 1'-0"

T.P.O. ROOF MEMBRANE
TAPERED RIGID ROOF INSULATION
¾" OSB SHEATHING
16" TJI w/ CELLULOSE INSULATION
1/2" GYP. BOARD
(x3) 9 ¾" 2.0E LVL
STEEL SADDLE
¾" GWB
STEEL COLUMN

3 DETAIL
A320 SCALE: 1" = 1'-0"

T.P.O. ROOF MEMBRANE
TAPERED RIGID ROOF INSULATION
¾" OSB SHEATHING
16" TJI w/ CELLULOSE INSULATION
¾" OSB SHEATHING
2x4 FUR OUT (FOR HVAC)
1/2" GYP. BOARD
DOBLE TOP PLATE, TYP.
¾" OSB NAILED FOR SHEAR
¾" GYP. BOARD
2x6 BEARING/SHEAR WALL

4 DETAIL
A320 SCALE: 1" = 1'-0"

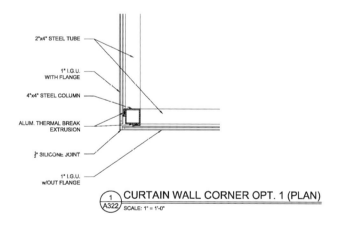

2"x4" STEEL TUBE

1" I.G.U.
WITH FLANGE

4"x4" STEEL COLUMN

ALUM. THERMAL BREAK
EXTRUSION

½" SILICONE JOINT

1" I.G.U.
w/OUT FLANGE

1 CURTAIN WALL CORNER OPT. 1 (PLAN)
A322   SCALE: 1" = 1'-0"

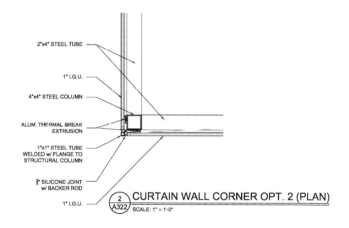

2"x4" STEEL TUBE

1" I.G.U.

4"x4" STEEL COLUMN

ALUM. THERMAL BREAK
EXTRUSION

1"x1" STEEL TUBE
WELDED w/ FLANGE TO
STRUCTURAL COLUMN

½" SILICONE JOINT
w/ BACKER ROD

1" I.G.U.

2 CURTAIN WALL CORNER OPT. 2 (PLAN)
A322   SCALE: 1" = 1'-0"

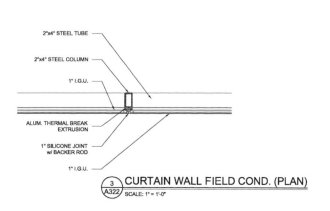

2"x4" STEEL TUBE

2"x4" STEEL COLUMN

1" I.G.U.

ALUM. THERMAL BREAK
EXTRUSION

1" SILICONE JOINT
w/ BACKER ROD

1" I.G.U.

3 CURTAIN WALL FIELD COND. (PLAN)
A322   SCALE: 1" = 1'-0"

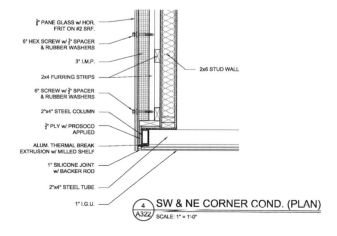

⅜" PANE GLASS w/ HOR.
FRIT ON #2 SRF.

6" HEX SCREW w/ ¾" SPACER
& RUBBER WASHERS

3" I.M.P.

2x4 FURRING STRIPS

6" SCREW w/ ¾" SPACER
& RUBBER WASHERS

2"x4" STEEL COLUMN

¾" PLY w/ PROSOCO
APPLIED

ALUM. THERMAL BREAK
EXTRUSION w/ MILLED SHELF

1" SILICONE JOINT
w/ BACKER ROD

2"x4" STEEL TUBE

1" I.G.U.

2x6 STUD WALL

4 SW & NE CORNER COND. (PLAN)
A322   SCALE: 1" = 1'-0"

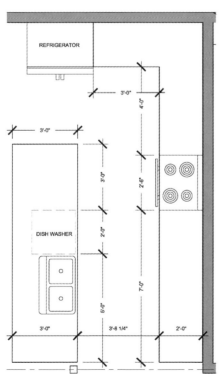

REFRIGERATOR

3'-0"

4'-0"

3'-0"

3'-0"

2'-6"

DISH WASHER

2'-0"

7'-0"

5'-0"

3'-0"

3'-8 1/4"

2'-0"

1
A130

ENLARGED PLAN

SCALE: 1/2" = 1'-0"

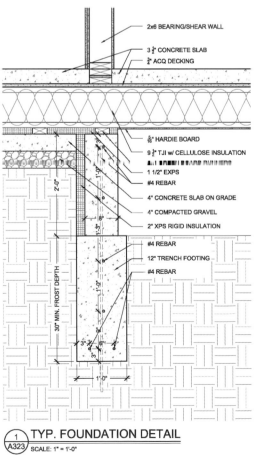

2x6 BEARING/SHEAR WALL

3 ½" CONCRETE SLAB

¾" ACQ DECKING

⁵⁄₁₆" HARDIE BOARD

9 ½" TJI w/ CELLULOSE INSULATION

~~~~~~~~~~~~~~~~~~

1 1/2" EXPS

#4 REBAR

4" CONCRETE SLAB ON GRADE

4" COMPACTED GRAVEL

2" XPS RIGID INSULATION

#4 REBAR

12" TRENCH FOOTING

#4 REBAR

1 **TYP. FOUNDATION DETAIL**
A323 SCALE: 1" = 1'-0"

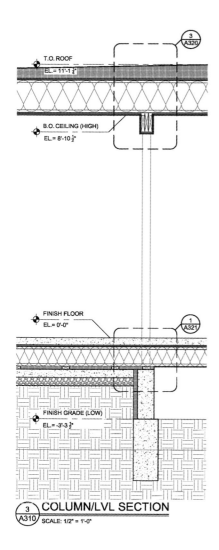

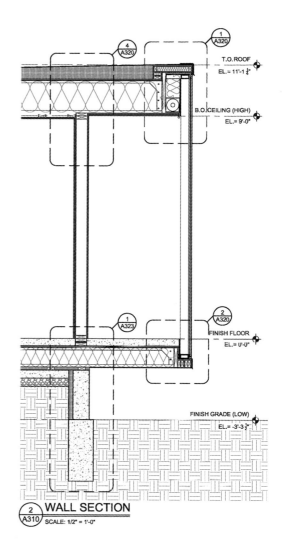

T.O. ROOF
EL.= 11'-1 ¾"

B.O. CEILING (HIGH)
EL.= 8'-10 ½"

FINISH FLOOR
EL.= 0'-0"

FINISH GRADE (LOW)
EL.= -3'-3 ¾"

3 / A310 COLUMN/LVL SECTION
SCALE: 1/2" = 1'-0"

T.O. ROOF
EL.= 11'-1 ¾"

B.O. CEILING (HIGH)
EL.= 9'-0"

FINISH FLOOR
EL.= 0'-0"

FINISH GRADE (LOW)
EL.= -3'-3 ¾"

2 / A310 WALL SECTION
SCALE: 1/2" = 1'-0"

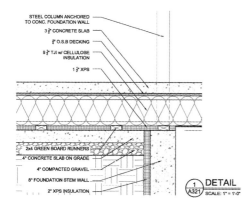

STEEL COLUMN ANCHORED TO CONC. FOUNDATION WALL
3 ½" CONCRETE SLAB
⅞" O.S.B DECKING
9 ½" TJI w/ CELLULOSE INSULATION
1 ½" XPS

2x4 GREEN BOARD RUNNERS
4" CONCRETE SLAB ON GRADE
4" COMPACTED GRAVEL
8" FOUNDATION STEM WALL
2" XPS INSULATION

1 / A321 DETAIL
SCALE: 1" = 1'-0"

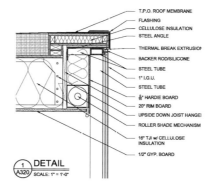

T.P.O. ROOF MEMBRANE
FLASHING
CELLULOSE INSULATION
STEEL ANGLE
THERMAL BREAK EXTRUSION
BACKER ROD/SILICONE
STEEL TUBE
1" I.G.U.
STEEL TUBE
⅝" HARDIE BOARD
20" RIM BOARD
UPSIDE DOWN JOIST HANGER
ROLLER SHADE MECHANISM
16" TJI w/ CELLULOSE INSULATION
1/2" GYP. BOARD

1 / A320 DETAIL
SCALE: 1" = 1'-0"

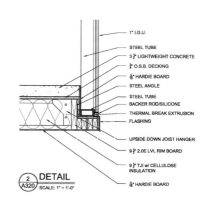

1" I.G.U.
STEEL TUBE
3 ½" LIGHTWEIGHT CONCRETE
⅞" O.S.B. DECKING
⅝" HARDIE BOARD
STEEL ANGLE
STEEL TUBE
BACKER ROD/SILICONE
THERMAL BREAK EXTRUSION
FLASHING
UPSIDE DOWN JOIST HANGER
9 ½" 2.0E LVL RIM BOARD
9 ½" TJI w/ CELLULOSE INSULATION
⅝" HARDIE BOARD

2 / A320 DETAIL
SCALE: 1" = 1'-0"

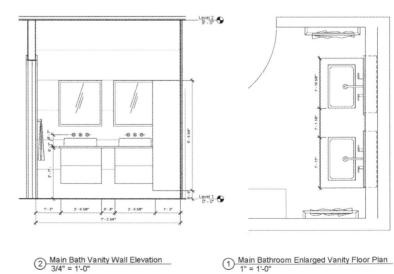

② Main Bath Vanity Wall Elevation
3/4" = 1'-0"

① Main Bathroom Enlarged Vanity Floor Plan
1" = 1'-0"

THE PRESENT AND THE FUTURE

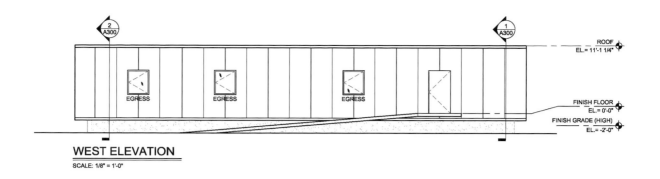

WEST ELEVATION
SCALE: 1/8" = 1'-0"

ROOF
EL.= 11'-1 1/4"

FINISH FLOOR
EL.= 0'-0"

FINISH GRADE (HIGH)
EL.= -2'-0"

EGRESS EGRESS EGRESS

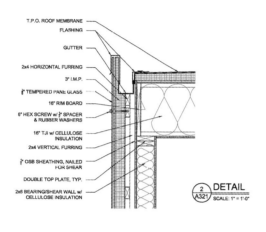

T.P.O. ROOF MEMBRANE
FLASHING
GUTTER
2x4 HORIZONTAL FURRING
3" I.M.P.
3/8" TEMPERED PANE GLASS
16" RIM BOARD
6" HEX SCREW w/ 1/2" SPACER
& RUBBER WASHERS
16" TJI w/ CELLULOSE
INSULATION
2x4 VERTICAL FURRING
1/2" OSB SHEATHING, NAILED
FOR SHEAR
DOUBLE TOP PLATE, TYP.
2x8 BEARING/SHEAR WALL w/
CELLULOSE INSULATION

2 DETAIL
A321 SCALE: 1" = 1'-0"

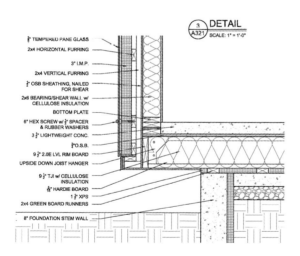

3/8" TEMPERED PANE GLASS
2x4 HORIZONTAL FURRING
3" I.M.P.
2x4 VERTICAL FURRING
1/2" OSB SHEATHING, NAILED
FOR SHEAR
2x6 BEARING/SHEAR WALL w/
CELLULOSE INSULATION
BOTTOM PLATE
6" HEX SCREW w/ 1/2" SPACER
& RUBBER WASHERS
3 1/2" LIGHTWEIGHT CONC.
3/4"O.S.B.
9 1/2" 2.0E LVL RIM BOARD
UPSIDE DOWN JOIST HANGER
9 1/2" TJI w/ CELLULOSE
INSULATION
5/8" HARDIE BOARD
1 1/2" XPS
2x4 GREEN BOARD RUNNERS
8" FOUNDATION STEM WALL

3 DETAIL
A321 SCALE: 1" = 1'-0"

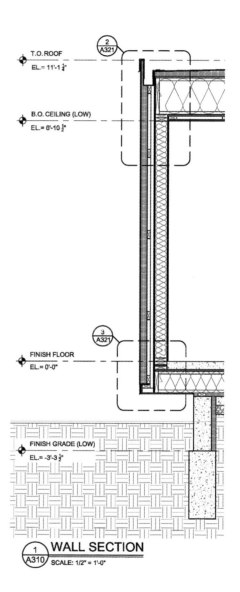

T.O. ROOF
EL.= 11'-1 3/4"

B.O. CEILING (LOW)
EL.= 0'-10 1/2"

FINISH FLOOR
EL.= 0'-0"

FINISH GRADE (LOW)
EL.= -3'-3 1/2"

1 WALL SECTION
A310 SCALE: 1/2" = 1'-0"

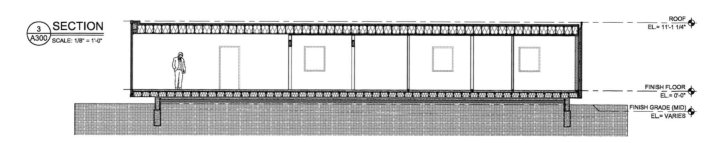

3 SECTION
A300 SCALE: 1/8" = 1'-0"

ROOF
EL.= 11'-1 1/4"

FINISH FLOOR
EL.= 0'-0"

FINISH GRADE (MID)
EL.= VARIES

Cantilever details and reinforcement

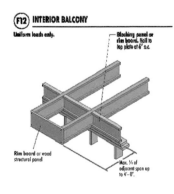

(F12) INTERIOR BALCONY

Uniform loads only.

Blocking panel or rim board. Nail to top plate at 6" o.c.

Rim board or wood structural panel.

Max. ¼ of adjacent span up to 4'-0".

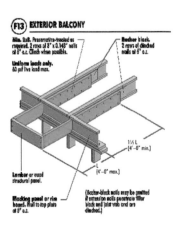

(F13) EXTERIOR BALCONY

Min. 3x8. Preservative-treated as required. 2 rows of 3" x 0.148" nails at 3" o.c. Clinch when possible.

Uniform loads only. 60 psf live load max.

Backer block. 2 rows of clinched nails at 6" o.c.

1½ L (4'-0" min.)

L (4'-0" max.)

Lumber or wood structural panel.

Blocking panel or rim board. Nail to top plate at 6" o.c.

(Backer-block nails may be omitted if extension nails penetrate filler block and joist web and are clinched.)

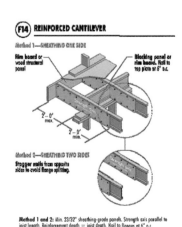

(F14) REINFORCED CANTILEVER

Method 1—SHEATHING ONE SIDE

Rim board or wood structural panel

Blocking panel or rim board. Nail to top plate at 6" o.c.

2'-0" max.

2'-0" min.

Method 2—SHEATHING TWO SIDES

Stagger nails from opposite sides to avoid flange splitting.

Method 1 and 2: Min. 23/32" sheathing-grade panels. Strength axis parallel to joist length. Reinforcement depth = joist depth. Nail to flanges at 6" o.c.

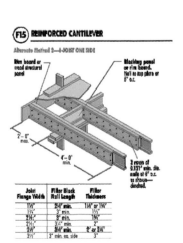

(F15) REINFORCED CANTILEVER

Alternate Method 2—I-JOIST ONE SIDE

Rim board or wood structural panel

Blocking panel or rim board. Nail to top plate or 6" o.c.

2'-0" max.

4'-0" min.

2 rows of 0.131" min. dia. nails at 6" o.c. as shown—clinched.

Joist Flange Width	Filler Block Nail Length	Filler Thickness
1½"	2½" min.	1¼" or 1½"
1¾"	3" min.	1½"
2¼"	3" min.	1½"
2½"	3¼" min.	2"
2¼"	3¾" min.	2" or 2¼"
3½"	3" min. ea. side	3"

THE PRESENT AND THE FUTURE

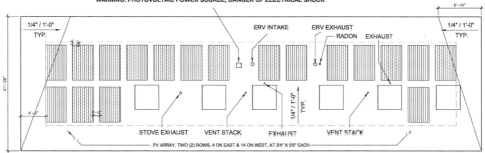

JUNCTION BOX FOR PV CONDUCTORS, PROVIDED WITH FOLLOWING WARNING LABEL:
WARNING: PHOTOVOLTAIC POWER SOURCE, DANGER OF ELECTRICAL SHOCK

1/4" / 1'-0"
TYP.

ERV INTAKE   ERV EXHAUST
RADON   EXHAUST

1/4" / 1'-0"
TYP.

1/4" / 1'-0"
TYP.

STOVE EXHAUST   VENT STACK   EXHAUST   VENT STACK

PV ARRAY, TWO (2) ROWS, 4 ON EAST & 14 ON WEST, AT 3'4" X 5'6" EACH

ROOF PLAN
SCALE 3/16" = 1'-0"

NOTE: SOLAR PHOTOVOLTAIC SYSTEM WILL BE
INSTALLED IN ACCORDANCE WITH 2014 NEC

METHOD OF ATTACHMENT: UNIRAC RM10, FLAT ROOF MOUNTED SYSTEM

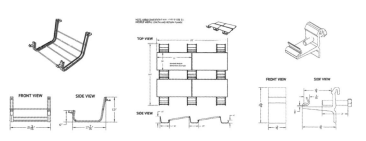

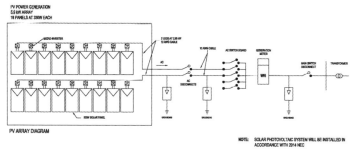

THE PAST | CLASS GROUP
PHOTOS AND STUDENT NAMES

The students who have been part of Studio 804

"Studio 804 is an amazing once in a lifetime experience that you never want to do again while it's happening but is strangely missed once you're gone". AJ Dolph, The Class of 2014.

THE BARBER SCHOOL 1995

Damien McBride
David Hinsley
David Vance
Dorinda Von Tersch
Georgia Gavito
Jitendra Kashyap
Joe Nocella
Kevin Stephenson
Lane Ikenberry

Lee Ann Duckett
Mark Hunter
Omar Chahin
Pam Dawson
Rick Dana Schladweiler
Rob Valenti
Sally Gibbs
Sie Mei Hwie
Tim Nielsen

THE McCREA STUDIO 1996

David Hinsley
Frauke Goldammer
Joe Nocella
Kevin Eckert
Lee Ann Duckett
Peter Boltres
Rick Catron
Seth Guthrie
Thomas Kaldewey
Tim Nielsen

THE MARVIN YARD CANOPY 1997

Amy Anderson
Casey Shook
Duane Cash
Florian Scheytt
Gregor Gimmel
Joseph Remick
Kee-Keat Tan
Lan Yan

Marc Bertolino
Marika Worthington
Michael Smith
Samuel Beckman
Tobias Gilk
Wendy Bagley
Zahir Poonawala

933 PENNSYLVANIA STREET HOUSE 1998

Anthony Denzer
Jason Hebert
K. Curt Shontz
Kim Wilson
Kristin Reisinger
Scott Smith
Theodora Bachorova
William Owings

1144 PENNSYLVANIA STREET HOUSE 1999

Aaron Olson
Jennifer Martin
John Stuckey
Jon Riddle
Julia Mathias
Kevin Ebersole

Kim Albrecht
Kristen Klint
Laura Sommers
Lauralynn Bodle
Miranda Grieder
Tara Alber

216 ALABAMA STREET HOUSE 2000

Allison Davidow
Amber Harden
Barry Boneau
Brett Anderson
Chris Kliewer
Cyrus Taleshi
Diane Rodriquez
Jacqueline Weston

Joe Lee
Laura Friesz
Lee Brooks
Michael Finder
Russell Zung
Steve Salzer
Tim Vetter
Tom Trenolone

RANDOM ROAD HOUSE 2001

Alexis Phillips
Billy Williams
Brenda Brosa
Chad Bristow
Jamie Fisher
Jessica Bristow
Joe Keal
Lou Nunez

Mark LaMair
Mike Miller
Mike Rosso
Nathan Rapp
Rene Goethel
Ryan Warman
Scott McMurray
Susan Regier

ATHERTON COURT HOUSE 2003

Brian Garvey
Brian Spainhour
Carl Drafall
Chris Boehne
Christina Assmann
Christine Prescott
Diane Mansfield
Dirk Henke
Erin Shea
Evan Fox

Frank Louis
Izumi Kitajima
Jean Dodd
Jessica Fishback
Kevin Gillian
Kyle Unruh
Lindsey Erickson
Lindsey Piant
Mike Schaefer

MOD 1 2004

Adam Gumowski
Anne Painter
Brian Finan
Brooke Knappenberger
Danielle Brooks
David Parks,
Gregory Keppel
Haylle Chau
Jeff Goode
Jen Dewitt

Kai Raab
Kevin Mut
Michael Haas
Nathan Couch
Nick Owings
Tony Onesti
Troy Ramirez
Wade Gardner
Will Robarge
Zack Allee

MOD 2 2005

Amy Stecklein
Basil Sherman
David Kelman
Griff Roark
Jess Weaver
Joe Davidson
John Howerton
John Schlueter
Kylee Lashley

Leann Vesecky
Mark Elsensohn
Matthew Bradley
Mike Gonos
Randy Taylor
Ryan Burton
Scott Clark
Stephen Elwood
Tony Lackey

MOD 3 2006

Amanda Langweil
Arjun Bhat
Brandon Crain
Brian Belcher
Bryant Bronson
Edward Hurtig
George Manis
Gil Akos
Jason Hartman
Jessica Braker

Jessica Deem
Jill Wendorff
Jonathan Holley
Karla Karwas
Lisa Reed
Michael Warner
Nathan Rosemann
Rachel Lin
Samuel Shepherd
Trevor Chalmers

MOD 4 2007

Brady Mark
Brent Kroner
Chris Wahl
Dani May
Eric Schlickman
Jonathan Kauffman
Kyle DeHaven
Lawren Jaccaud
Lincoln Lewis
Lindsey Cunningham
Matt Friesleben

Michael Cook
Mitchell Brown
Nate Mast
Nate Otis
Nick Adams
Pat Knobloch
Ryan O'shea
Ryan Walters
Suzanne Petersen
Ted Arendes
Zack Cole

547 ARTS CENTER 2008

Abby Henson
Boyd Johnson
Chris Clark
Corey Davis
Corey Russo
Erik Heironimus
Jenny Kivett
Jessica Buechler
John Gillham
John Tarr
Josh Somes

Justin Cratty
Katie Rietz
Krissy Buck
Lindsey Evans
Mark Cahill
Megan Thompson
Sarah Boedeker
Simon Mance
Tim Overstreet
Will Lockwood
Zack Arndt

3716 SPRINGFIELD STREET HOUSE 2009

Alison Lampier
Andrew Thomas
Becca Maness
Benjamin Chapman
Blake Perkins
Caleb Reed
Collin Jacobs
Danielle Blodgett
Erik Biggs
Frank Lindemann
Garret Wilson

Jared Eder
Jason Sadler
Jesse Brubacher
Joshua Bender
Kate Frick
Kyle Davis
Megin Rux Sevier
Molly Fogarty
Patrick Noble
Sam Edelstein
Stephanie Winn

PRESCOTT PASSIVE HOUSE 2010

Aaron Jensen
CJ Armstrong
Colleen Driver
Daniel Lipscomb
Daniel Matchett
Elizabeth Beckerle
Jennifer Mayfield
Joel Garcia

Joshua Brown
Katherine Morell
Laura Foster
Lauren Hickman
Matthew Johnson
Tye Zehner
Tyler Harrelson
William Doran

CENTER FOR DESIGN RESEARCH 2011

Allison Pinkerton
Andrea Kirchhoff
Andrew Younger
Ashley Banks
Ben Shrimplin
Ben Welty
Brian Winkeljohn
Cade Brummer
Dan Schaeffler
Gerard Alba
Giannina Zapatini
James Ice

Jenny Kosobud
John Myers
Justin McGeeney
Kate Penning
Kirsten Oschwald
Mandi Miller
Mariah Tooley
Matt Holderbach
Michael Mannhard
Michael Prost
Sarah Brengarth

GALILEO'S PAVILION 2012

Aaron Aday
Adam Smith
Andy Seemiller
Chris Claassen
Dan Nordmeyer
Jon Hanes
Kevin Porter
Liz Pritting
Megan Carrithers

Melissa Schoch
Nate Jarvis
Phil Meyer
Raymond Dwyer
Rhett Morgan
Seamus McGuire
Stephanie Stone
Thomas Nguyen

ECOHAWKS, THE HILL ENGINEERING
AND DEVELOPMENT CENTER 2013

Ashlee Burleson
Bryan Stockton
Elizabeth Avenius
Hannah Hindman
Hayder Alsaad
Hunter Hanahan
Kate Medin
Kelli Hawkins
Mandy Moore
Mark Hageman

Mark Zeitler
Matt Patterson
Matthew Bethel
Max Anderson
Melanie Arthur
Mike Kelly
Owen Huisenga
Rachel Mattes
Ryan Barry
Ryan Shults

THE FORUM AT MARVIN HALL 2014

Aaron Sirna
AJ Dolph
Alyssa Sandroff
Ben Peek
Christine Harwood
David Versteeg
Ian Heath
Jonathan Wilde
Jordan Goss
Josh Ostermann

Ken Grothman
Krista Cummins
Kyle Kutz (Summer)
Michael McKay
Nathan Brown
Nicolas Elster
Renee Brune
Sara Lichti
Tim Ostrander

1301 NEW YORK STREET HOUSE 2015

Alex Wolfrum
Andrew Forney
Connor Rollins
Dustin Adler
Jake Banton
Karsten Erdman
Khanh Le
Kim McKeever

Maria Guerrero
Mariam Al-taweel
Melody Refaat Benyamen
Nick Stinebrook
Patrick Reuter
Pia Westen
Sam Florance
Zac Dawson

1200 PENNSYLVANIA STREET 2016

Abby Henson
Boyd Johnson
Chris Clark
Corey Davis
Corey Russo
Erik Heironimus
Jenny Kivett
Jessica Buechler
John Gillham
John Tarr
Josh Somes

Justin Cratty
Katie Rietz
Krissy Buck
Lindsey Evans
Mark Cahill
Megan Thompson
Sarah Boedeker
Simon Mance
Tim Overstreet
Will Lockwood
Zack Arndt

1330 BROOK STREET HOUSE 2017

Abigail Rose Davis
Brittany C Hediger
Caitlin Fitzgerald
Charles Christian Rotter
Chris Roybal
Emily Renee Stockwell
Evan Taylor Liles
Faysal Karim Bhuiyan
John Joseph Coughlin
Matthew Phillip Anderson

1220 E. 12TH STREET HOUSE, 2018

Alexa Kaczor
Austin Bosecker
Ben LaRue
Danielle Latza
Elayna Svigos
Eric Pincus
Erik Erdman
Hanu Madireddy
Ian Mutschelknaus

Joe Schaefer-Glick
Kevin Purdom
Linda Emilson Cotter
Mark Romanoff
Wes Seaba
Will Ehrman
Will Siegel
Zach Lundgren

GRADUATE ESSAYS

Thoughts about Studio 804 from those who survived

CJ Armstrong | Chicago, Illinois | Prescott Passive House, 2010

Before I joined Studio 804 I had had the opportunity and privilege to work with a large firm in Chicago as part of the design team on many large-scale projects in Shanghai, Dubai, Abu Dhabi, Istanbul, Seoul and several projects in the US. They ranged from mixed use skyscrapers to several million-square-foot residential complexes, hospitals, schools and museums. While I learned a great deal during this period, there Is a very specific reason I chose Studio 804 as a graduate program.

After an architectural education, which consisted of countless design studios and structural/graphic design/research classes, something was still missing. As my professional career was blooming something still seemed missing. What I found in Studio 804 which I have not been able to find before is confidence; the confidence to stand up among the architectural community and defend the work I helped produced as important.

Alex Wolfrum | St Louis, Missouri | 1301 New York Street House, 2015

Each new class of Studio 804 has thought that no other project was as difficult as theirs, and for my class that was equally true. Every year starts off the same way, with professor Dan Rockhill and an inexperienced group of students sitting in "the box" at the University of Kansas' unmarked warehouse East of Lawrence. There they learn from past projects and brainstorm ways to improve upon them. This is the process that led our class to attempt both a USGBC LEED Platinum-rating, and Passive House Institute US certification for our building, a house that would also meet requirements for the new Living Building Challenge Net Zero certification.

Before getting to this, our class committed several months to finishing the previous year's project, The Forum at Marvin Hall, spent a week in New Orleans at the Greenbuild convention, then a few more searching for a suitable site. Midway through construction of the 1301 New York house, we took another week to prep for Studio 804s 20th anniversary Symposium, which drew in Studio 804 alumni and like-minded architects from around the country. It was only fitting to hold it in the warehouse amid an installation of reclaimed glulam beams, donated to the program by Olson Kundig Architects. In our "free time" between those projects we managed to design a house to the highest of energy efficiency standards. We owe much to the Studio 804ers who came before us and set the bar so high. Only by building on their templates for research, design, and construction could we achieve our own success.

One of the most important steps in the Studio 804 formula is the sourcing of materials. Dan likes to say that we use the "whole buffalo" and in keeping with this sustainable mantra our class foraged through the warehouse. It was amazing to see the mountain of assorted insulation left from previous years dwindle to nothing as we built our R-65 Frankenstein. When the well ran dry, partner companies donated what we needed to flesh out the 1301 New York House, adding value and interest to our educational experience. No Studio 804 project would be possible without them. Then came the real challenge: assembling the parts. More than cutting and nailing, it's about gaining the confidence to make that first cut and drive that first nail. This is the unique experience that Studio 804 thrives on. The format pushes you outside of your comfort zone to a place where accelerated learning can happen. The intense satisfaction is a feeling I'll be looking for the rest of my architectural career.

Hayder Alsaad | Baghdad, Iraq | EcoHawks, 2013

I've studied architecture and architectural engineering for six years. In that time, I experienced all types of studios: architectural, urban, landscape, and interior design. These classes focus on major issues architects face, such as the design concept, function, structure, and materially. Yet, they neglect those things that dictate design in the real world: budget, building codes, and mechanical systems. Studio 804 is a great method of learning. Students must consider every aspect of the building and make details work, because they must build them. Any miscalculation in design will lead to bigger problems during the construction process. The real world, hands-on experience is what makes Studio 804 the richest learning experience a student can possibly receive. My favorite part was the problem solving. Dealing with construction problems and trying to figure out what to do instantly and build it the right way is amazing. Understanding the concept of design tolerance is fundamental to what we did: the real world is not as exact as the CAD world. Building materials are not perfect. That's why Studio 804 is different from other teaching programs; it taught us to be smart, to account for everything, and to try to anticipate the problems we might face before they occur.

Studio 804 stresses the importance of teamwork, working with professionals and problem solving. Having 20 students with various visions requires a high level of teamwork to reach the best possible design, and to coordinate the work of all the students to build it as fast as possible. Working with our consultants was a great opportunity to interact with professionals in the fields of structure, mechanical, electrical, and plumbing.

Many people ask me why I did it. I am not going to be a builder; I am not going to end up cutting steel, screeding concrete or framing walls for my projects. This is true, but to come up with a successful detail, it is necessary for an architect to know how the different parts will come together. There is no better way to learn this than to design a detail and to test its constructability for yourself in a real situation. I am an international student, which makes my background different than American students. There are many cultural differences between us, which made the experience even more interesting. It was a great honor to be able to share my ideas and techniques with my classmates, and to show them how to do things in what Professor Rockhill likes to call "the Iraqi way. "Being part of the Studio 804 family was a great chance to meet new people, master the language, and learn about a different culture. It was an experience that I will remember for the rest of my life.

Krissy Buck | St Louis, Missouri | 5.4.7 Arts Center, 2008

As a studio, we often joke of Professor Rockhill's different phrases of encouragement. It was not until we endured the numerous discussions about the smallest detail, the endless hours spent on the phone with product suppliers, shoveling outside while it was pouring down rain, and pushing a 7,000-pound mod just a few inches, that we truly understood that "good work takes hard work". I remember the tremendous amount of work that needed to be done, but never doubting our ability to get it done. Every person researched their respective area of expertise and soon could present their knowledge akin to a professional of the same field. This transformation is merely one display of Dan's teaching ability. I saw 21 other people, with the same passion and dedication as myself, grow together.

We had the opportunity to build something that not only would we remember for the rest of our lives, but something that carried significant meaning to an entire city. In Greensburg, our sustainable prototype serves the community as their 547 Arts Center. By playing an integral part in their rebuilding efforts, we have set an example for others to follow. Our project will offer inspiration and provide a place for people to gather, share their artistic views, and be reminded that art can bring us together. Though I started with what I thought to be a good grasp on the building process, I found this grasp to be somewhat biased and limited. I can say with certainty, I left my final year at the University of Kansas with a much more comprehensive view of the architectural practice due to my involvement with Studio 804.

Benjamin Peek | St Louis, Missouri | The Forum at Marvin Hall, 2014

The Forum at Marvin Hall was a very special project from its inception. A vision between the School's Dean and Dan Rockhill spawned ten years prior seemingly could have never come to fruition without the collaboration of the University of Kansas' Studio 804; a special task and challenge indeed. Despite unforeseen submissions, delays, misfortunes, and re-submissions that seemed to hold the project in limbo from day one, Dan Rockhill would always tell us, "We have a building to build." Rockhill and Studio 804 taught us to take each stride as a lesson to alleviate the pains of the next. This is how one makes the impossible possible. This Studio 804 class thrived based on this mantra. Bringing together 18 naive graduate students not only to design but build a building within the confines of one year seems impossible? Not for Studio 804. An experience, an education, and a tradition unmatched by any other program in the world proved an idea could become reality with staunch academic curiosity and venture.

For myself, Studio 804 revealed a layer in architecture that traditional academia never touched on; the real world and its variabilities. Prior studios allowed me to detach architecture from real difficulties and the technicalities of a complex and somewhat non-linear building process. The context of Studio 804 allowed me to ask: how are buildings constructed, with what material and what must happen simultaneously in the background? In my opinion, architecture became much more interesting when these complexities unveiled themselves and were confronted. This is what Studio 804 represented for me. Dan Rockhill has become so meticulous with his technique for teaching that the building became a by-product of the immense knowledge set we gained throughout the year. The journey was by no means tranquil. The ride was one of ups and downs, through which many personal and group trials and triumphs occurred; it is an experience so entrenched in error that it was sometimes hard to discern what constituted success or progress or even failure.

The idea that students would design and build a building on their very own campus is wild. The fact that architecture students did build an addition to their existing architecture school is verging on an absurdity. Nevertheless, the final product was a great team achievement but the real reward came with every painstaking day required to reach that goal. It is impossible to put into words all the things I learned from this undertaking and the values Dan Rockhill has instilled. It is an experience that can only be understood first-hand, and understood through doing.

Jared Eder | Aitkin, Minnesota | 3716 Springfield Street House, 2009

I like to compare my Studio 804 experience to an Outward Bound trip. Outward Bound takes a group of young people and places them into situations they would never otherwise find themselves. Often, reluctantly, rock climbing, canoeing, cooking over a campfire, the list goes on. Boundaries are pushed and horizons broadened. Just committing to the trip takes guts and self-evaluation. Taking a leap that lands you far from your comfort zone and places you in the unknown is often a life changing experience, one I would guess most people do not experience.

Studio 804 took 22 students and planted them firmly into the unknown with one common goal in mind, to design and build a ground-breaking architectural gem with an impossible time line. Led by professor Rockhill we were guided along the right path but never shown the way. We were placed deep into that proverbial wilderness and told to find our own way out. We were all in this together. Personal boundaries both physical and psychological were tested daily. Soon those boundaries began to recede. Inevitably there comes a time when you find yourself doing something you had never done before and would have never dreamed of attempting. Those are the moments when you really stop to take stock of what is going on around you and how valuable the experience is.

The technical skills and building knowledge gained with Studio 804 are an invaluable part of any architectural education. However, and maybe most importantly, you learn how to work effectively in a team, how to teach, how to listen, how to com-

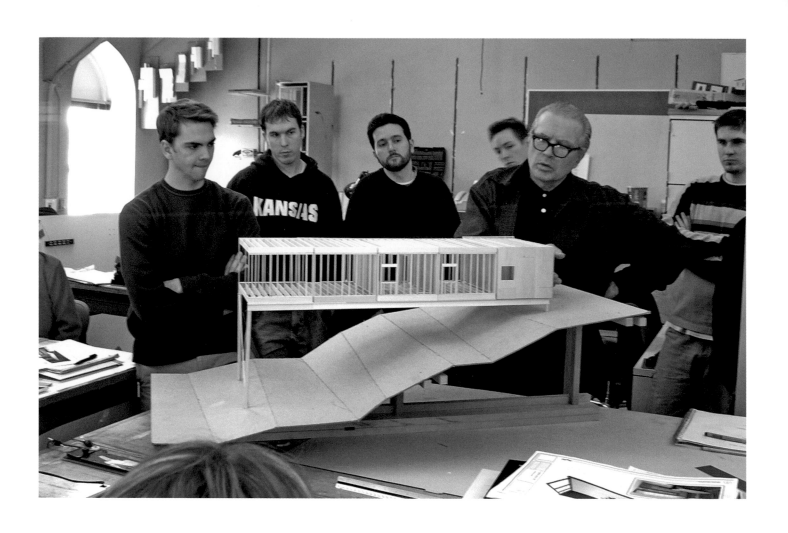

municate, and how to compromise. The roles of teacher and student are interchangeable when you are placed in a situation that requires creativity and collaboration. In life, we all need to be pushed to really know who we are and what we are capable of. We were pushed to our limits and then some, now it is up to us to not forget what we can do

Sam Florance | Aledo, Texas | 1301 New York Street House, 2015

After completing a few small-scale design build projects in my undergraduate architectural studies, I quickly learned the value of hands-on experience. It also became apparent how this mode of learning was largely neglected in the academic world. When selecting a graduate school, I sought out a program that would embrace a hands-on/real-world learning experience and I found Studio 804 to be the fulfilment of that. I came to the University of Kansas with high expectations for Studio 804, all of which were surpassed. Professor Dan Rockhill takes the work his studio produces very seriously and creates a professional environment for his students which I found to be refreshing after being in many lax studios. Studio 804 is a truly comprehensive experience where we as students are responsible for all aspects of building, from design and budgeting to pouring concrete and framing walls. However, the lessons learned in Studio 804 go far beyond the architectural realm into team dynamics and work ethic. When you are expected to produce a full scale, LEED Platinum, Passive, Net Zero house in such a short amount of time you have no choice but to work together as a team and to find the common ground with fellow classmates that will get the job done. It is a sweet moment in Studio 804 when the group is firing on all cylinders and work gets done quickly and efficiently. Professor Rockhill even coined a phrase for these times in the Studio, he calls it "The Swarm". The valuable lessons learned in this studio are too many to count, but it should suffice to say that this experience has had a profound impact on my education.

Pia Westin | Seattle, Washington | 1301 New York Street House, 2015

When it comes to design build programs around the country, I think Studio 804 is about as good as it gets. Few who see the work 804 has produced believe that it's all student built, beginning to end. I spent a good chunk of time researching all the different design build programs around, and I think 804 is the most comprehensive, developed, and sophisticated one out there. You would be hard pressed to find another program that has met LEED Platinum and PHIUS standards, not to mention doing so year after year. Everything is done by Dan and the students from start to finish, including project procurement, securing donations, design, sourcing materials, permitting, accounting, and of course every aspect of construction. While everyone comes in with varying degrees of work experience and construction know-how, there is not much, if any, favoritism placed on what you come in with. It was my experience that the amount of responsibility given to each student is dictated by work ethic and initiative, two things I think Dan respects and cultivates in students. It's not about who you are or what you know when you start, but the time and effort you commit to learn the things that you don't.

Dan is not the hand holding type. He expects you to figure things out on your own, using him as a resource once you can hold an intelligent conversation about a topic. He also likes to say that Studio 804 is not for everyone, a warning that he has high expectations for both quality and quantity of work, and is not afraid to tell you when you're wrong, lazy, or an idiot. The time commitment and criticism, though warranted, is what seems to be the biggest adjustment for people starting out, and something that takes a little getting used to. If you don't have a thick skin now, you'll certainly have one by the end. It's a long, exhausting year with early starts and long days, but also a lot of fun and absolutely worth the effort. The list of things you'll learn both from the work, and especially from Dan, not only about construction and design, but also about managing a team, a schedule, a budget, a site, and a practice is just about endless.

As far as integration into practice goes, Studio 804 was the smartest move I could have made, as the skills and experiences that I gained in 804 set me apart from other applicants as well as my co-workers. 804 nurtures and develops a tenacious and efficient work ethic, and the fundamental difference between drawing a detail and putting it together is apparent and tremendous. It's been my experience that principals appreciate a young architect who can hold an intelligent conversation about detailing, construction sequencing, cost, and creative problem solving, and reward it with added responsibility and better projects.

Brittany Hediger | St. Louis, Missouri | 1330 Brook Street House, 2017

Throughout my years at KU, everyone talked about how intense and demanding Studio 804 is. I'd have to agree that it was nothing short of that, but I wouldn't change my experience for the world. This program is the most valuable exposure you can get to the built environment during your education. It unequivocally prepares you for the architectural profession. In a short ten months, you learn how to work through all facets of design and construction from concept development to the final product. The opportunity to work as a team with classmates and Dan Rockhill to produce a physical space that demonstrates the culmination of all our hard work is one of the most rewarding aspects. I will forever miss my time spent in Studio 804 and will continue to joke that my architectural career may have peaked before it even started because of this experience.

Matthew Anderson | Denver, Colorado | 1330 Brook Street House, 2017

Of all the options I had for choosing a graduate program, I chose The University of Kansas because of Studio 804. You will sweat till you can wring your shirt out, and you will work in cold enough weather hand warmers do absolutely nothing. Professor Dan Rockhill's teaching style will force you to do things you didn't think you were capable of. All of this is what yields a result that few Architecture programs in the country can truly boast. I would even say I learned as much about myself as I did about the architectural building and construction process.

11

APPENDIX

DAN ROCKHILL

ACSA and JL Constant Distinguished Professor of Architecture,
University of Kansas, School of Architecture and Design.
The Association of Collegiate Schools of Architecture,
Distinguished Professor, 2014.
Executive Director, Studio 804, Inc., University of Kansas.
Owner of Rockhill and Associates.

CREDITS

DAVID SAIN
Architect with Rockhill and Associates since 1988.
Adjunct Lecturer at The University of Kansas.

JAMES EWING/OTTO PHOTOGRAPHS
 EcoHawks, The I lill Engineering and Development Center: pages
224-225, 232, 234-237, 239, 245, 248 (below right), 251, 252-253.
- The Forum at Marvin Hall: pages 2-3, 14, 258 (above), 261, 262,
269-272, 273 (above), 276, 277 (above), 284-285.

COREY GAFFER PHOTOGRAPHY
-1330 Brooks Street House: 314-316, 318-322, 323 (below),
324-325, 328-331, 333, 335 (above).
-1220 East 12th Street House: 347, 354-379, 388-395.

ACKNOWLEGMENTS

The students who have participated in Studio 804 deserve the biggest thanks. It takes a tremendous commitment at an early point in their lives as architects. I doubt I would have been able to easily do the Studio 804 boot camp when I was their age. I hope each one has eventually seen the rewards of experiencing a trial by fire. I have no doubt it takes some time for the discomfort, the long days, and my constant demands to fade in the memory and be overtaken by memories of working with their classmates to produce something special.

Kent Spreckelmeyer and Dean John Gaunt, are colleagues at the University of Kansas who have backed me from the beginning. They helped me start and shape the program. Studio 804 would never have developed into the educational program it is without their wise support and advice.

When Studio 804 became a not for profit corporation I had to form a board of directors. All the individuals who have served have been supportive while respecting the autonomous way I am required to run the program. I thank them for their time and consideration.

Before Studio 804 came to be I was working with students in my practicum class to build things. It took a supportive and vocal faculty member like Harris Stone to champion this work. He recognized the value of the course and felt it fitting for university students to leave the classroom, get out in the field and get dirty. His encouragement was essential as the program continued to evolve and become something unique to architectural education.

For over twenty years my wife and family have put up with my working many hours every day while also keeping a business afloat. Thank you for suffering through a lifetime of a distracted husband and father.

At the beginning of each year I let the students know that there will be thousands of photographs taken during the duration of the project. It is impossible to give credit to each photographer when we share our work. If a student puts a photo in the mix the credit they will receive is "courtesy of Studio 804." In nearly every instance I have been the photographer of the finish photography but I have had students produce some spectacular images over the years. CJ Armstrong, Aaron Aday, and Caleb Reed are prominent examples - there are others. James Ewing of James Ewing/OTTO has produced some of the beautiful images of The Forum at Marvin Hall and EcoHawks. Corey Gaffer contributed inspired images of the 1330 Brook Street and 1220 12th Street houses. Hobart Jackson, Charles Linn, and Matt Kleinmann are colleagues who also have taken photos of our work that has been included in this book.

Thanks to Retro Inferno's Rob Parks for his generosity in allowing me to cherry pick the furniture and curiosities in his Kansas City store. Year after year his inventory brings the appropriate style to the projects as I work on the finish photography.

I thank the students who took the time to reflect on their experience and provide the essays used in the book.

Doug Callahan, has been a Rockhill and Associates employee for about half the Studio 804 years and has occasionally been a tremendous help.

I could not have done this without David Sain. We set up a system where I would sit on the phone on a job site and talk about whatever project or issues was the focus of that days writing. He would record my ramblings and hone the random thoughts into intelligent chapters, often bringing his own observations to the mix. We have worked together in Rockhill and Associates for nearly thirty years and share a common belief in the value of hard work and a determination to let little stand in the way of achieving our creative goals. David's dedication to everything we have worked on has propelled me to be better in many ways and I am indebted to him.

SELECTED AWARDS

LEED Platinum Certified, USGBC
- 1220 East 12th Street House, 2018
- 1330 Brook Street House, 2017
- 1200 Pennsylvania Street House, 2016
- The Forum at Marvin Hall, 2016
- 1301 New York Street House, 2015
- EcoHawks, The Hill Engineering and Development Center, 2014
- Galileo's Pavilion, 2013
- The Center for Design Research, 2012
- Prescott Passive House, 2010
- 3716 Springfield Street House, 2009
- 5.4.7 Art Center, 2008

Passive House Institute, US (PHIUS) Certified
- 1301 New York Street House, 2016
- Center for Design Research, 2012
- Prescott Passive House, 2010

2016
- Canadian Wood Council, Wood Design Award, The Forum at Marvin Hall
- AP Systems Design Award, 1301 New York Street House
- St Louis Architect and Designer Awards, 1301 New York Street House

2015
- Best of 2015 Design Award, Architect's Newspaper, November

2014
- Central States AIA Design Award for Excellence, The Forum at Marvin Hall
- Finalist, AZURE Design Award, EcoHawks, The Hill Engineering and Development Center
- Architizer Design Award, EcoHawks
- Association Collegiate Schools Architecture, Distinguished Professor

2013
- Fassa Bortolo Italian Award for Sustainable Architecture. Honorable Mention. Galileo's Pavilion
- Engineering News-Record. Best Projects: Green Project. Merit Award. Galileo's Pavilion
- Honorary Senior Fellow Inductee 2013, Design Futures Council

2012
- Kansas American Institute of Architects (AIA) Award, The Center for Design Research (CDR) and Galileo's Pavilion
- Honorable Mention, International Prize for Sustainable Architecture 2012
- Construction Specifications Institute Sustainable Education 2012 Award KC
- Design Intelligence, Noted as one of the thirty top architectural educators in America, 2012 Report

2011
- Holcim Awards, Acknowledgement Prize for North American Architecture, The CDR
- Dan Rockhill, Cooper-Hewitt National Design Award Finalist in Architecture
- Evergreen Award, Greenhouse Award, Architect Magazine, 3716 Springfield House
- Residential Architect Design Awards, Grand Award, Single Family Housing, Mod 4
- Grand Award, Studio 804, Residential Architect, Design Awards

2010
- International Wood Products Association (IWPA), Environmental Excellence Award, Springfield House
- Central States AIA Design Award, St Louis October 2010 Prescott House
- Residential Architect Design Awards 2010, Merit Award, Lolomas, NM
- Watermark Award, Honoring Excellence in Kitchen Design, 2010

2009
- National Council of Architectural Registration Boards (NCARB) Prize for Creative Integration of Practice and Education in the Academy
- Green Good Design Award, European Center for Architecture Art Design and Urban Studies and Chicago Athenaeum: Museum of Architecture and Design, Mod 4
- Environmental Protection Agency (EPAs), Lifecycle Building Challenge, Honorable Mention, 5.4.7 Art Center
- Education Honors Award, AIA, Studio 804

2008
- Eco Structure, Evergreen Award, Honorable Mention, Mod 4
- Into the Open: Positioning Practice, Venice Architecture Biennale, Venice, Italy
- Wood Design Award, Wood Design & Building Magazine
- Residential Architect Design Awards 2008, Merit Award, Nest House
- Residential Architect Design Awards 2008, Merit Award, Platform House

2007
- Dan Rockhill, Cooper-Hewitt National Design Award Finalist in Architecture
- EPAs Lifecycle Building Challenge, Honorable Mention, Mod 3
- Boston Society of Architects, In the Pursuit of Housing, Mod 3
- Residential Architect Design Awards, Judge's Award, Mod 3
- Decatur Modern Design Challenge, Award Winner, Mod 4
- Residential Architect Design Awards, Judge's Award, Mod 3
- Residential Architect Design Awards, Merit Award, Kansas Longhouse

2006
- Architect Magazine, Home of the Year Award, Mod 3
- Architecture Magazine's 'Home of the Year Award', Platform House
- Residential Architect Magazine, 2006 Firm of the Year Award
- CSI, Gold Award for Excellent Craftsmanship, Mod 3
- Ferrous Park, International Design Competition, First Award

2005
- Boston Society of Architects, In the Pursuit of Housing, Sp 2005

2004
- Architect Magazine, Home of the Year Award, Mod 1
- Wood Design Award, Wood Design & Building Magazine

2003
- NCARB Prize for Creative Integration of Practice and Education in the Academy
- Graham Foundation for Advanced Studies in the Fine Arts, Grant recipient, Contemporary Interpretations of the Kansas Vernacular Landscape: The Work of Rockhill and Associates, support for exhibition

2002
- Design Build Institute of America, Distinguished Leadership Award
- Dwell Magazine, Modernist Award, Anniversary Issue
- Dragonfly House Award, American Concrete Institute, KS chapter
- Wood Design Award, Wood Design & Building Magazine

2001
- The David Award, Archeworks, Chicago, Excellence in Design for People with Disabilities, Third Place Award, Random Road House
- Design with Memory, International Competition for Sustainable Design, First Place, Random Road House
- World Architecture Awards, Finalist, 216 Alabama House
- Residential Architect Design Awards, Judges Award, 216 Alabama House
- First Place Award, Association of Collegiate School of Architecture (ACSA) Steel Tube Competition, Studio 804, 1603 Random Road
- Kemper Fellow, Distinguished Teaching Award, University of Kansas

2000
- Design Matters, Best Practices in Affordable Housing, City Design Center, Chicago, 216 Alabama House
- AIA, Livable Communities Award, Studio 804, 216 Alabama, September
- Residential Architect Design Awards, Grand, Affordable Housing, 1144 Pennsylvania

SELECTED PUBLICATIONS

2018
- Grable, Juliet. Net-Zero in the Heartland, Home Power, Jan Feb
- Editors, Top Schools, University of KS Studio 804, Azure, Jan Feb

2017
- Keegan, Edward. 1330 Brook St, Architect Magazine, September
- Stonorov, Tolya. The Design-Build Studio: Crafting Meaningful Work in Architecture Education, November
- Corner, et al. Prescott + NY Passive Houses, Passive House Details
- Schittich, Christian."The Forum at Marvin Hall," Architecture +Urbanism Glass Façade, Japan, August
- Transsolar, Bioclimatic Construction, High Comfort-Low Impact, DETAIL Germany, Issue 5
- Transsolar, Bioclimatic Construction, High Comfort-Low Impact, DETAIL, English edition, Vol. 4

2016
- Kraus, Chad. Editor "Work Ethic, Ethical Work," Designbuild Education
- Aksamija, Ajla, "Center for Design Research, University of Kansas", Integrating Innovation in Architecture, United States
- "A Forum for Practical Learning". Green Building and Design, March, April

2015
- Hill, David, "Study Hall". Architectural Record Magazine, November, pp 140-145
- Gerfen, Katie, "Learning Curve", Custom Home Magazine, May
- Wilmes, Adam, "Studio 804". Altruism by Design, United Kingdom,
- Lentz, Linda, "Dynamic Glass". Architectural Record Magazine, March
- "Net Zero Passive House". Greenability Magazine, Spring
- Zamora Francesc. "Springfield House". 150 Best Sustainable Designs

2014
- "Field Guide to Architectural Education". Azure November/December
- Bell, Victoria Ballard. "Center for Design Research". Materials for Design 2, United States
- Hand, Gunnar. "DIY Lecture Hall," Architects Newspaper, August
- Dabkowski, B. "Illuminating Aluminum," Design Bureau 100, Summer
- Groom, Sean. "Breeding Grounds, Studio 804," Fine Homebuilding Sp
- Editors, 547 Art Center, Kansas Travel Guide, Kansas Magazine, Sp

2013
- Gerfen, Katie. "EcoHawks Research Facility". Architect Magazine, August
- Moskovitz, Julie Torres. "Prescott House". The Greenest Home: Super insulated and Passive House Design, United States

2012
- "Energy Efficient University Building". Third Holcim Awards, Sweden
- Lovric, Vladimir, "Eco House", ekokuca Magazine, Serbia, June
- Tsiora-Papaioannou, Dimitra. "Epeynhtiko Kansas", Ktirio, Greece,
- Serrats, Marta, "1000 Tips by 100 Eco Architects: Guidelines on Sustainable Architecture from the World's Leading Eco-Architecture Firms", Canada
- Serrats, Marta, "Modular 4", Prefab Houses DesignSource, United States
- Van Uffelen, Chris. "Prescott House", Passive houses: Energy Efficient Homes, United Kingdom

2011
- Wu, Yang, "Sustainable Residence – 3716 Springfield", Atlas of World Architecture, United Kingdom
- Goodman, Jennifer, "Affordable Housing Goes Green", Residential Architect Magazine, December
- Nyary, Erika. "Epiteszhallgatok Passzivhaza," Alaprajz Magazine, Hungary, December
- Duran, Sergi Costa, "3716 Springfield", "Sustainable Prototype: Arts Center", Source Book of Contemporary Green Architecture, United States
- "Greensburg 547", Ktipia Magazine, Greece, Spring
- Aquilino, Marie J., "Greensburg", Beyond Shelter: Architecture and Human Dignity, United States
- Phaidon Press, "Sustainable Residence", Phaidon Atlas of 21st Century World Architecture," United Kingdom

2010
- Mays, Vernon. "Superinsulated House", Architect Magazine, September
- Dickinson, Elizabeth Evitts, "Facing the Numbers", Architect Magazine, September
- Chang, Sun Ah. "Sustainable Residence", Interni Magazine, Korea, June
- Bahamon, Alejandro and Sanjinés, Maria Camila, "Random Road", Rematerial: From Waste to Architecture, United States
- "Gjenbruk og innovasjon I Kansas", Arkitektur Magazine, Norway, October

2009
- Grisel, Julien. "Le Studio 804, Recyclage et Construction", Traces: Number 18, Switzerland
- Ejlertsen, Matilde. "Greensburg: More than Just a Name", Award Magazine, Volume 2, Number 7, Australia
- Purkayastha, Devyani. "Dan Rockhill Studio 804", Indian Architect & Builder, India. September
- Schoof, Jakob. "Neubeginn in Platin". Detail Green Magazine, Germany, February
- Tilder, Lisa and Blotstein, "Studio 804", Lisa, Design Ecologies: Essays on the Nature of Design, United States
- Sokol, David. "Best Green Houses", GreenSource Magazine, December
- Duran, Sergi Costa. Prefab Houses, Germany
- Fabris, Luca Maria Francesco, "Il prototipo fa scuola", Costruire Milano Magazine, Italy, April
- "Mod 4", Contemporary House, Germany

2008
- Duran, Costa Sergi, "547 Art Center", New Prefab, United States
- Bahamon, Alejandro and Sanjinés, Maria Camila, "Random Road", Rematerial Del desecho a la arquitectura, Spain
- Galindo, Michelle, "Mod 3+4", 1000x Architecture of the Americas, United States
- Zacks, Stephen. "Whirlwind Tour", Metropolis Magazine, November
- Kiendrebeogo, Gildas. "Apres la tornade", Ecologic Magazine, France, October
- Linn, Charles. "547 Arts Center, Kansas", Architectural Record, October
- Sokol, David. "Teaching by Example", Architectural Record, Oct
- Sokol, David. "Students help rebuild Greensburg", Architectural Record

2007
- Trulove, James and Cha, Ray "Mods 2+3", PreFab Now, United States
- Roberts, Charlene. "Modular 3", Innovative Home Magazine, June
- Ferjancic, Ivan. "Houses Biointeligentno", Hise magazine, Slovenia, May
- Norman Blogster. "Portrait of Studio 804", Mark magazine, Number 8, The Netherlands
- "Mod 3", Arquitectura y Diseño magazine, Spain, May

2006
- Cramer, James, "Mod 3", Almanac of Architecture and Design, United States

2005
- Sparkes, Ken. "Prefab", Spaces, London, September
- Suning, Fan. "Modular I House", Tsinghua University Architecture Publications, China, April
- Lecuyer, Annette. "Studio 804", DeArchitect, Netherlands, April 2005

2004
- Bussel, Abby "Prefabricated Modular House", Architect Magazine, April
- Grady,Mark. "Snapshot: Dan Rockhill," The Zweigletter, August 2004

2003
- McGraw, Hesse. "Studio 804", Review, Architecture

2002
- Archer-Barnstone, Deborah. "Building Designs for Living: Studio 804 University of Kansas", Journal of Architectural Education, February

BOOK CREDITS

Carter, Brian. Editor, Design & Building: Rockhill and Associates.
Introduction by Juhani Pallasmaa, Postscript by Todd Williams.

Art Director: Oscar Riera Ojeda
Graphic Design: Lucía Bauzá

OSCAR RIERA OJEDA
PUBLISHERS

Copyright © 2018 by Oscar Riera Ojeda Publishers Limited
ISBN 978-1-946226-21-1
Published by Oscar Riera Ojeda Publishers Limited
Printed in China

Oscar Riera Ojeda Publishers Limited
Unit 4-6, 7/F.,
Far East Consortium Building,
121 Des Voeux Road Central, Hong Kong
T: +852-3920-9312

Production Offices | China
Suit 19, Shenyun Road,
Nanshan District, Shenzhen 518055
T:+86-135-5479-2350

www.oropublishers.com | www.oscarrieraojeda.com
oscar@oscarrieraojeda.com